Photojournalism:
A Freelancer's Guide

Photojournalism:
A Freelancer's Guide

Harvey L. Bilker

Contemporary Books, Inc.
Chicago

Library of Congress Cataloging in Publication Data

Bilker, Harvey L.
   Photojournalism: a freelancer's guide.

   Includes index.
    1. Photography, Freelance.   2. Photography, Journal-
istic.   I. Title.
TR690.2.B54   1981   778.9′907   81-65188
ISBN 0-8092-5919-2   AACR2
ISBN 0-8092-5918-4 (pbk.)

Published by Contemporary Books, Inc.
180 North Michigan Avenue, Chicago, Illinois 60601
Manufactured in the United States of America
Library of Congress Catalog Card Number: 81-65188
International Standard Book Number: 0-8092-5919-2 (cloth)
                                    0-8092-5918-4 (paper)

Published simultaneously in Canada by
Beaverbooks, Ltd.
150 Lesmill Road
Don Mills, Ontario M3B 2T5
Canada

For my wife, Audrey, and our son, Scott

Contents

Acknowledgment

I wish to thank all the editors who have shown interest in my photography for the often extraordinary creativity they have applied to the selection, cropping, and layout of my pictures.

Most of the news and feature photographs in this book which have been published have appeared in *The New York Times, Star-Ledger* (Newark, New Jersey), *Asbury Park Press* (New Jersey), through the Associated Press wire, and in magazines, and local tabloids.

In accordance with each publication and wire service's policy regarding pictures submitted on speculation, assigned, or reprinted, I own the negatives and rights to these specifically selected photographs.

Introduction: Seeing Your Own Pictures in Print

Anyone can sell a photo to a newspaper—as long as the photographer knows how. Editors are more open to buying outside photographs than most people think. But to sell, you wonder, does the picture have to be a professional shot, extraordinary in subject, perfect in exposure and composition?

No. Those are the rare exceptions—the photos you occasionally see on a major daily's front page, those sent to your local paper by a wire service, or those you read about in photography books.

Do you have to have a darkroom? No, you don't. With a minimum of inexpensive equipment and materials—and without a darkroom—you can present an editor with professional negatives. With just a little more equipment, you can produce a proofsheet. Of course, it does help to have a darkroom. But, on the other hand, an editor who is anxious to see what pictures you have might have your film developed on the spot.

There are many, many large newspapers in cities across

America and Canada, and even more local tabloids, that would welcome spot news photos from you.

First, let's consider the average news photo.

Not all automobile accidents, fires, and other news incidents that occur in a particular area can be covered by the local newspapers. No matter how many staff photographers a newspaper has, it is virtually impossible to have on-the-spot coverage at every happening.

In addition to the news, regularly employed newspaper photographers have to shoot scheduled events such as sports, groundbreakings, awards, parades, and meetings, as well as feature pictures to accompany stories written by reporters about local people and situations. And there are even times when two or more news incidents happen simultaneously and only one staff photographer is available in that area. Because of this, these staff press photographers are often unavailable—and even unreachable—when a newsworthy event suddenly occurs. When it does, the whole thing could be over before a photographer arrives on the scene. In the case of an accident or other disaster, emergency personnel are quick to arrive at the scene and handle the problem, whether it involves taking an injured victim to a hospital or flipping an overturned car back onto its wheels. By the time an editor learns of such a situation and sends a photographer, the drama that might have been captured on film may be gone forever. In addition, when all the staff photographers are tied up, an editor often will hire freelancers to cover routine events.

An automobile accident or a fire in which a person is killed or seriously injured is often relegated to a few paragraphs inside the newspaper if there is no picture of the tragedy. But it can become front page news should a picture be available. It is a known fact that the photo above the front page fold in a newspaper has a great influence on sales. And, in turn, a high circulation attracts advertisers. So editors are always looking for exciting news shots.

Other incidents that occur—and at which there are no photographers—also make interesting photographs. Look through your local paper carefully, in detail, and take note of them. Houses collapse, private planes land on highways, areas are seriously flooded after heavy rain, lightning strikes a building or tree, cars run into houses, businesses are picketed, bank robbers are caught, riots are started, celebrities pass through town, dogs and cats have to be rescued, a truck might hang off a bridge, or a child might get a finger caught in a bike—and there are numerous other events of an interesting nature. When the story is told by a picture, the reader's curiosity is aroused and the accompanying caption or article read.

But spot-news pictures are not the only photos that a newspaper will buy. They will sometimes purchase scenic shots of your area, such as beaches during the summer, fireworks displays, crowds at fairs or parades, and eye-catching photos of other local scenes.

It is also possible that after you have proven your capabilities to an editor you will be given assignments to cover scheduled events such as local high school sports, a political speech, a dedication of a bridge, students at a science fair, or any number of other situations.

Newspapers are not the only publications that buy photographs from freelancers. Photos can also be sold to magazines. In many instances, these sales can be reprints—spin-offs of your sales to newspapers. More details on this appear later.

Press photography can be done as a sideline to provide excitement, artistic pleasure and satisfaction, and extra income. It can also eventually become a full-time job.

Many photography hobbyists don't care for chasing after fires or other such news events. Others are unable to go to news happenings because of commitments to a full-time job. Whatever the case, these shutterbugs can still have the pleasure of seeing their photo work in print—possibly with their names credited, not to mention the resultant income. For these people, the sale of photos is still possible. Newspapers and magazines do buy pictures other than spot-news photos from freelancers. Keep in mind that the magazines most commonly known to the average person are those on the newsstand, and these periodicals buy primarily from experienced and established photographers. However, there are hundreds of magazines being published regularly that are not as visible. Company house organs and trade publications buy thousands of photographs from photographers who, though they may not be professionals, show professionalism in their work.

If you are interested in selling freelance photos, this guide will tell you how to achieve that goal. It will provide you with how-to information that can help you make it happen.

This book will tell you how to work with what camera equipment you already have. If you are considering buying replacement equipment or additional equipment, you will find hints that will aid you in choosing what is best for you.

The purpose of this guide is to provide information ranging from taking spot-news photos to getting them into the editor's hands—and into print. It also covers a great deal of ground in between. You will learn whether a newspaper will process your film, and if so, when. It will tell you how to develop film yourself—fast. You will also find darkroom hints on special processing for bad lighting conditions, details on how to dry your negatives quickly and safely, and other developing pointers.

Along the way, this book will give you tips on how to get the best pictures at a news incident and what kinds of film and lenses you should use for different situations and conditions. Some other important facts detailed include what caption information you should get, how to set your camera, what angles are best to shoot, and how to get the radio signals of police, fire, and first aid teams. You will also find facts on who owns the photo negative and copyright after you sell your picture, where to find a treasury of magazine markets, and how you can sell the same photo more than once.

Contained in these pages are numerous photos that I actually had published in newspapers and magazines. In addition, pictures that I have taken especially for instructing you in freelance photography are also included.

And, for fun—to test your news photo intuition—I have

added a picture quiz section. You will be shown the pictures of single news events that I turned in to the editors. After making your guess as to which were bought and published, you will be able to check your answers against the correct ones.

Another feature that I have included is called "How *Not* to Take Press Pictures—Trial and Error." These picture comparisons of the wrong and right way to cover an event show blunders I have made in both technique and judgment. Its purpose is to help you avoid making the same mistakes.

Also, you will find numerous photos that I took, both published and unpublished, with explanations of how I obtained them.

This book will take you behind the scenes with me for a glimpse of my experiences in photojournalism. I hope that, as a result, those of you who have doubts about selling your work will be encouraged to try. Making sales to your local paper—or at least getting them published, as a starter—is not as difficult as you may think, provided your goal is approached properly.

This guide will explain how to accomplish your photojournalistic objectives. In addition, it will tell you how to go about finding extra markets.

Always remember that the newspaper editor wants to be close to the people. That's what journalism is all about. The editor tries to reach each individual reader. He or she also wants to be reached in return, whether by a letter of response for the editorial page or through other contributions—and that includes photos taken by a reader that other readers would enjoy sharing. The door is regularly open for the photojournalist, whether experienced or not, with that first interesting picture.

Age makes no difference in the sale of freelance newspaper photos. Neither does occupation. You can be of school age or retirement age. It is what you have on your film that counts. It can be a way of making some money or a means of letting editors know that you are a good photographer and that you are available. Finally, it is a means of getting your foot in the door for full-time employment.

I made my first sales, when I was a teenager, to the *Philadelphia Inquirer* and *Philadelphia Bulletin*. One of those pictures was a shot of a car-trolley accident that happened across the street from my father's hardware store. I shot the picture from the second-story window of the business of one of the family's friends. (I would have had a picture of the car jammed between *two* trolleys, but the window hadn't been opened for years and by the time we got it loose one of the trolleys had been moved.) The other photo I sold was of a five-car collision on a bridge, which I happened across while taking a high school camera club on a camera trip when I was the club president. By the way, another member of the club sold one, too—to the competing newspaper.

One important point: you should have your camera with you or immediately available at all times. If it is loaded, so much the better. When you spot an incident that has just occurred, there is usually not a moment to lose.

There are ways to be prepared so that you can put spot news on film quickly, efficiently, and effectively.

This guide will tell you how.

Photojournalism:
A Freelancer's Guide

1

You Are on the Scene by Chance

Imagine you are driving along a highway one morning. In the distance, you see emergency vehicles, their red lights twirling and blinking. There has been an accident. You have your camera with you. You'd like to take pictures and try to make a sale to a local newspaper.

Pull over to the side of the road, either before or beyond the site of activity, and park where your car will be well out of the way of emergency equipment that has arrived or may appear.

Get out of the car and go to the scene of the accident, being careful not to interfere in any way with the emergency teams who are carrying out their duties.

Look the situation over. See if you can ascertain exactly what has happened from a visual, photographic viewpoint. Did a car go down the embankment? Were two vehicles involved in a crash? Was a car or truck on fire?

If anyone engaged in emergency activities is momentarily available, ask what happened. Even a passerby can sometimes be of help.

Consider the lighting. At the same time, circle the scene of the accident at whatever points possible. Go as close as you possibly can. If you are asked to move back, do so. Always observe the rules set up by emergency people. Be cooperative and polite. Don't provoke those on duty; if you do, it may only work against you. Be professional in your behavior. People's lives may be at stake, and that is obviously more important than any picture.

In many instances you may not be able to get the picture you would like, but if you are the only photographer at a disaster scene, whatever pictures you take of the incident will be the only ones available, and odds are that there will be at least one market for what you have.

You might tell those in charge that you are taking a newspaper photo and that you are a freelance photographer. Sometimes just that fact will get you a brief opportunity to snap one or more pictures from a point near the scene of the incident. Letting one photographer get in close is not as obstructive as allowing a crowd to move in.

Record on a piece of paper the location and time of the incident. If you can get any other facts, such as names of the victims, do so. But that is not always possible under pressured conditions. Then go to the nearest phone.

If you are familiar with the names of the local newspapers, you know which to call. Otherwise, if you are in an area you don't know too well, you might be able to ask someone in the vicinity for the names of the papers that carry local news. At worst, the yellow pages will give you a list of papers to check.

Metropolitan newspapers are open almost around the clock. Call and ask for the news desk. Tell the person on duty that you would like to speak with someone who is authorized to buy news photographs.

When you have that person on the phone, tell him or her about the pictures you took, with facts about where and when the incident occurred and any other details you may have obtained. If you learned of any deaths or injuries—even if they sounded like rumors—detail that, too. The newspaper is in touch with local police and can check out facts—and such information will encourage them to look into the incident immediately, thereby increasing your chances for a sale.

If all goes smoothly, you will be invited to bring your film directly to the newspaper for developing. This, of course, would happen to you in an ideal situation. However, there are often many factors that interfere with or delay success. For example, the person you should speak with at the newspaper might be out to lunch or the newspaper may have sent its own photographer. Possibly, the paper may just not be interested, there may be no one at the office at that moment who can develop the film, or you may have missed the deadline. We will cover these points and many more as this book progresses.

First, let's start with camera equipment.

2

Is Your Camera Satisfactory
for News Photos?

From time to time a "classic" photo of poor quality depicting a major news event turns up on the cover of a national magazine or appears in newspapers across the country or even in publications around the world. It is somewhat out of focus, grainy, or of poor contrast. Still, it has impact.

Why does such an inferior picture command exceptional interest? Because it portrays an occurrence of monumental importance. Someone who happened to be there with a camera captured that instant for posterity. And although the subject was not defined sharply in the picture, there was enough of an image that a viewer could add to it with imagination. In addition, its lacks may convey a mood. Had no one snapped that picture at that time and place, no visual record at all would have been made for history.

Any camera, then, as long as it is used properly and produces a recognizable image, will usually serve your purpose. However, not all incidents are of such great notoriety that an inferior photograph might intrigue an editor.

5

Most cameras—even the most inexpensive—are capable of producing photos that are reasonable for newspaper reproduction. If you can take a clear picture with the camera you own, you can sell a news photo. But you must keep in mind that many inexpensive cameras are designed to take pictures only under ideal conditions. The more current low-priced pocket cameras, though, are capable of being set for slightly adverse conditions.

If you wish to photograph a spot-news event in which the light is not perfect, where there is action involving more than average movement, or where you must be unusually close, you must have a camera on which you can adjust the focus, aperture, and speed. You will need a camera that can be adjusted to take pictures under specific conditions. Problems with which you might have to deal include inadequate light— poor illumination, a subject with the light behind it, or the need for flash lighting greater than that which is provided by an automatic camera flash; a subject very close to the camera; or a person or object traveling at a rate that would blur in a shot taken by a camera having no speed settings, usually having a shutter that works at about 1/30 second.

The most versatile camera available today for press photography is the 35mm SLR (single lens reflex). This kind of equipment is manufactured by many companies and prices for it begin at very low levels. In fact, excellent bargains can be obtained when purchasing used ones. Camera stores often sell them for as little as half of what they would cost new, and sometimes a private party asks for less than half.

The 35mm SLR camera is commonly used by both amateurs and professionals because of its compactness and the availability of a wide variety of compatible films, lenses, filters, flash equipment, other accessories, and darkroom apparatus.

Naturally, the more you pay for a 35mm camera, the better the quality of the camera body and lens will be. But there is a point in this range of prices—at about the cost of a medium-priced camera—at which additional cost pays for greater flexibility in picture taking rather than quality of equipment. A good portion of the price of the more expensive 35mm

SLRs goes toward wider apertures, faster shutters, and built-in conveniences that save the photographer time, permitting a lesser reliance on memory and the need to make fast calculations. For example, cameras that can be put on what is called *aperture priority* can set exposure automatically. Such advantages are nice to have, but they are not a necessity. In fact, unless used with knowledge and skill, they can work to the detriment of the photographer. An aperture priority–adjusted camera aimed at a person in shadow against the sky will underexpose the subject if it isn't set for those special conditions.

The average, basic, functional 35mm camera is the one that can serve a photographer well for newspaper photographs. In the SLR viewfinder you see exactly what you will get, because when you depress the shutter button the mirror that shows you the lens's field of vision in the viewfinder flips up momentarily—to put that exact image on the film—then drops back down again. In addition, it has a through-the-lens metering system. This saves you the time of having to figure out the exposure after consideration of several factors— basically, the speed of the film, the light on the subject, and the shutter speed—that might otherwise require you to dig out the film's package circular for study.

There are other cameras besides the 35mm type whose formats, or negative sizes, would be suitable. These, too, range from reasonably priced units to expensive high-quality models. For example, there are the 2¼ x 2¼ reflex cameras and the 2¼ x 3¼ and 4 x 5 press cameras used by most newspersons many years back, before the 35mm camera became popular.

However, if you are currently planning to buy a camera, and you have intentions of trying to sell photos to newspapers, a 35mm SLR will be useful to you in other areas, too. It is ideal for family snapshots and travel pictures that can be taken with color slide film and projected for viewing. With it, you can also have color or black-and-white negative film made into enlargements in dimensions ranging upward from wallet size to 8 x 10 and much larger—with clarity.

In addition, most 35mm camera bodies will accept a change

of lenses. This gives the photographer many advantages. Close-ups can be taken from near or far with the use of regular and telephoto lenses. Wide-angle lenses can squeeze large scenes into a shot with the size of your subject exaggerated in the foreground.

Most newspaper darkrooms are set up primarily for 35mm processing, though they do have the capability of processing other formats.

In conclusion, then, any camera is right for you for news photos if you are shooting under good conditions and past experience has shown that you can obtain a good, clear photo under ordinary circumstances. But the most convenient all-around camera for the press photographer is the 35mm SLR. For that reason, this manual, when getting down to fine detail, will concern itself primarily with that type of equipment. Nevertheless, all the information offered here is applicable in general to all other cameras and formats.

In photojournalism there always has been and always will be a key factor whose importance transcends all camera equipment, materials, and technology, and that is the human element—the person behind the camera. It is the skill and judgment of the photographer, in the final analysis, that shapes the finished product with all of its excellence and flaws, its final artistic and even magical touch, permanently fixing an image that stops a point in time and space forever.

If you can produce a picture that you, as a newspaper reader, would want to see—both as an interesting news event and as a good photographic record of it—there is a good chance that an editor will want to buy it from you.

As you read on, you will learn what techniques will help you obtain professional results: what you should see in your viewfinder before snapping the shutter—and how to get it there.

Motor Drive/Auto Wind

Although motorized film-moving devices are not necessary,

they are extremely handy to have for news, sports, and other events. With use of them, however, comes the temptation to overshoot, which should be resisted. Whether or not you use this type of accessory, make every shot count. Duplicate what you have already taken only when you can improve on it, when interesting variations of the shot are occurring from which you might make a selection, or when a subject might have blinked at the time the shutter clicked.

Sometimes the activity in a scene can be in a constant state of flux, and one particular moment of many captured will be a gem. In such an ever-changing setting, snap at moments of peak interest, but don't just hold your finger on the motor drive button and hope for the best. A second is such a long time that an ideal moment may be lost unless you trip the shutter at that right instant, rather than wait until the motor drive comes up with the next snap a quarter of a second later.

The auto wind can save you precious seconds that can be put to use concentrating on the scene while holding your camera in the same position without interruption.

3
Lens Choices in Photojournalism

There is no agreement among photographers as to what is the best focal length for a lens to use for average shots. Focal length, which refers to the distance from the lens to the film when the camera is set at infinity, is not the same measurement as the dimension referred to for filters and lens shades— the diameter of the lens. The common consensus among professionals regarding what is a "normal" lens for a 35mm camera is one with a focal length of about 50mm. Still, there are some photographers who feel that a 35mm lens, which has a slightly wider angle of view, should be used in general photography.

Many different kinds of lenses are available today, the majority of which can be adapted to almost any camera. In fact, most companies specializing in lens manufacture will sell you a lens adapted at the base to whatever brand of camera you use. In some cases, adapters themselves are available.

Each year, as technology advances, dozens of new lenses appear on the market, and they are becoming increasingly lighter, sharper, and more sophisticated—and sometimes even less expensive than their predecessors.

Because many photographers, both amateur and professional, keep their purchases up to date with the latest trends in photo optics, you can benefit from the steady stream of lenses that are traded in for new ones. Many used-lens bargains are always available.

Is the quality of the lens important or are they all alike?

The expression *you get what you pay for* applies very definitely to lenses. Expensive lenses, for one thing, are given more attention by the manufacturers when they are ground. Therefore, higher-priced lenses have an advantage over cheaper ones because they produce more definition, especially when employment of their widest apertures makes use of their entire glass elements.

A lens of lesser quality, at its widest opening, will be more apt to put the scene at the edges of your picture out of focus, despite perfect focus at the center.

Much of the distortion produced by any lens can be avoided by using the smallest aperture possible for an exposure. Of course, the less light allowed into the camera, the lower your speed must be—or, the more sensitive, or faster, your film must be. These disadvantages in speed and grain potential must be weighed on every picture-taking occasion.

Wider lenses, which are designated by low numbers such as $f/2$ (as opposed to $f/4.5$), are more expensive. However, they can be of great advantage when that small amount of additional light for your film makes the difference between getting a picture and getting none at all. Such situations might present themselves at outdoor sports events, when the sky is overcast and it is imperative that you shoot at a fast speed; or indoors, when a speaker and large audience have to be photographed and the flash cannot light the entire area. The low f-number, or wide opening, also has disadvantages: a short depth of field occurs that requires careful focusing with a keen eye and precise fingering.

Lens coatings, which lessen light flare on your film, also figure into cost, as do lens barrels that don't tighten up in freezing weather, preventing aperture adjustment.

Built-in advantages are found in some lenses. In zoom lenses, the one-touch feature allows you to move your subject close and far in your viewfinder at the same time as you are focusing. Other lenses require that each function—zoom and focus—be handled separately. Such extensive adjustment activity during the rush of sports photography can result in pictures lost.

Some lenses, called *macro,* can provide extreme close-ups at short distances as well as from far away—a feature of some telephotos.

If you would like to have lenses in your bag to cover all contingencies of news photography, there are three basic types you will need: normal, wide-angle, and telephoto. You can, of course, branch off from there with the use of zooms in each of these categories. Or you can have intermediate fixed-focus lenses with wide *f*-openings in your collection.

You should always have your equipment packed and ready to go. The normal lens should be on the camera, and your other lenses should be stashed in your bag where you can get to them immediately. Usually, when you arrive at a news event, every precious second counts, and the scene may require a quick switch to another lens.

When you change lenses under the pressure of limited time, remember to be certain to return each one to your camera bag. Don't put them on a curb, table, floor, or the ground. You may never see them again.

For most somewhat distant spot-news happenings or features requiring a telephoto lens, such as sports or a fire in an upper-story window, 135mm is the length that should serve your purpose best. However, if you plan to buy a zoom telephoto, an ideal one would be in the 100–200mm range. It will give you that extra leeway you need on either side of 135mm.

If possible, always try to get "tight" shots of your subject. If you don't, you will have to crop, or mask out, the edges of the picture from the negative when printing it. And when you crop a photo, you lose detail from the remainder of the negative that you will blow up. A tight shot, however, is not always possible with a lens that has a fixed focal length; it is not always physically possible to move closer to, or farther away from, your subject. With a zoom lens, of course, a simple hand movement accomplishes this effect.

Certain sports can be photographed better with lenses longer than 200mm, ranging to 300mm, 400mm, 500mm, and more. For example, long lenses are best for shooting scull races with paddlers or speedboats from another craft anchored on the water. Extremely distant news scenes such as a person threatening to jump from a bridge or upper story of a building can also be better photographed by lenses longer than 200mm. But an editor realizes that spectacular shots such as these, even if they have to be enlarged considerably, are better than no pictures at all. And sometimes, paradoxically, an unclear picture resulting from graininess or imperfect focus adds to the drama of the event.

Available at a broad range of prices are various telephoto extenders, such as 2X and 3X, which multiply focal length. When a camera body and a 135mm lens are interfaced by a 2X extender, for example, telephoto power is increased to 270mm. At the same time, though, the light entering the camera is diminished. The f-number, with the use of a 2X extender, would have to be multiplied by 2; a normally used $f/8$ aperture would then become $f/16$. However, a through-the-lens metering system would automatically make the adjustment. These adapters also work on zoom lenses.

A wide-angle lens can provide you with many advantages in news and feature photography. If you are tightly packed in a group of photographers taking pictures of a number of people from close up, and you are unable to move back easily to include more of the scene in front of you in your viewfinder, a wider-angle lens than usual would be handy. Photographers who are in competition with others taking pictures of celebrities in a cramped area find that a 20mm lens, which is extremely wide, accomplishes this purpose. Some distortion will be produced at the edges of your photo, but you will, at least, have included all of your scene. Besides, the distortion sometimes adds an intriguing dimension to the picture.

Fish-eye lenses are extremely wide-angle lenses that cover views of as much as 180 degrees and more. In other words, they can actually "see" somewhat behind the sides of the camera. As an extreme example, a 6mm lens would cover 220 degrees. Such lenses, however, are needed only for special circumstances, and it is unlikely that you would be covering any of them as a freelancer. Should you have use for them, however, keep in mind that fish-eye lenses can be rented.

What, then, is the best focal length for a wide-angle lens for the photojournalist? This is a matter of personal preference. However, it should definitely be between 20mm and 35mm. The shorter the focal length, the more distortion of your view you will get, especially when the subject—whether human or inanimate—is close to the camera. You may personally desire extreme distortion—or you may not.

I use a 24mm lens. I find that it suits my wide-angle needs in general. In fact, I feel that my investment in this focal length with a maximum aperture of $f/2$ has paid off considerably. I have used it often under bad lighting conditions with excellent results.

An important advantage of a wide-angle lens is that it provides an extreme depth of field. When focused on a person at a distance neither extremely far nor very near, the normal or telephoto lens, using an average f-opening, will put objects before and behind that person out of focus. With the wide-angle lens, on the other hand, you can have everything simultaneously in focus—from a head-and-shoulders close-up of a person to mountains in the distance—even when the aperture is set at maximum.

A wide-angle lens is often useful for photographing auto accidents because you can move in close to a victim being removed on a stretcher by first aid people and at the same time include the damaged vehicles and ambulances. Additionally, your center of interest will be slightly exaggerated in size. And there are many other scenes that can benefit photographically from this kind of wide-angle close-up.

Naturally, the more lenses you have, the more different ways you can photograph an event. On the other hand, extra lenses also mean more equipment to lug around, to make decisions about, and to root through when you're in a hurry.

But, if at the present time you are considering only the bare essentials needed for press photography, you will be well equipped for just about anything that can turn up when you have those three important lenses: normal, wide-angle, and telephoto.

4

Which Films You Should Use—and When

Black-and-White

A press photographer's camera should always be loaded, its film speed indicator in the position corresponding to that film. It is also a good idea to have the shutter speed set at a commonly used speed of about 1/100 second or 1/125 second. Your lens aperture should be close to what would be needed at that speed on an average day. Then, when you arrive at a scene where there is action in progress, you can whip out your camera and, with a minimum of adjustment, begin taking pictures.

Naturally, your camera should be loaded with film that will serve you best under all light conditions, including the worst. You can always switch to other films from your camera bag if you find you have the time. However, if you can't spare the seconds, you will still be able to take pictures with a fast film.

Press photographers find a high-speed film (ASA 400) most useful. Should you find, on your arrival at a newsworthy scene, that the existing light is extremely bright, as on a blindingly sunny day, and you have time to replace your fast film, a good average emulsion to use is one with an ASA rating of about 100 or 125.

If you do not have enough time to replace your fast film, just increase your shutter speed to about 1/500 second. This will give you a combination of disadvantages and advantages—and the disadvantages can be overcome.

The main disadvantage is that you will have more grainy negatives than you would have had with a lower ASA film if it is subsequently developed in a fast developer, which most newspapers use. But keep in mind that when your picture is finally screened into dots for engraving and transferred to newsprint, the loss will not be that noticeable. Besides, fast film and fast developer will produce pictures of high contrast, which will compensate for any lost detail.

Although film processing in a freelance photojournalist's own darkroom or at a newspaper photo lab is usually done with a fast developer, there are fine-grain developers that will prevent loss of detail and take only five or ten additional minutes to use. But if you are delivering raw, or undeveloped, film to a newspaper to be processed, its darkroom may not have a fine-grain developer on hand—or if it does, it may not be mixed, and you will have to have your negatives developed in their standard solutions. Some large-circulation newspapers use a machine that will produce completely developed, fixed, and dried negatives from your roll in about eight minutes. The quality of the results depends on the chemicals used, the condition of the machine, and the skill of the person developing the film.

An advantage of using high-speed film in bright sun conditions is that you will be able to shoot at a small aperture of $f/16$ or $f/22$. This will give you a maximum depth of field, allowing you to obtain sharp focus from a reasonable foreground distance to the background. Should you find that certain views of the scene you are photographing are in shadow, you will be able to set your speed back to about 1/100 second (because of the high ASA sensitivity) and continue without the interruption of changing film.

A planned event, such as an outdoor festival, will allow you the time to select a film that is more suitable for existing light conditions. You may even want to obtain extremely fine detail with the use of a very slow, fine-grain film (ASA 25). This will permit you to obtain special effects. A film rated at a low speed requires considerable light, which will allow you to use a wide aperture. This means that you will be able to take a close-up picture of a person and throw the background out of focus. Fine-grain film will also give you delicate shadings in outdoor portraiture.

For shooting under available light, which is explained in another chapter, an ASA 400 film is a good all-around kind to work with. It can be used to achieve artistic effects indoors with either artificial or natural light—or both.

Film speeds can be jacked up through the use of specific developers or special formulations of normally used chemicals. Certain developing solutions are designed to produce fine-grain negatives in addition to increasing the ASA rating.

An ASA 400 film can be "push"-processed to an incredible 3200—and even higher. But in such extreme cases, special attention must be paid to the lighting on the subject. However, most poorly illuminated available light scenes can be photographed successfully within an ASA range of 800 to 1200, or even up to about 2000.

There are wide varieties of films and chemicals for push-processing, and your local camera store proprietor can help you determine which are best for you. In addition, manufacturers of film and chemicals will be pleased to send you literature regarding this use of their products.

Knowledge of this area of press photography is important to the photojournalist. Many news happenings have to be shot under extremely inadequate light conditions. Yet, if you think out all aspects of film, lighting, and developing before shooting, you can come away with exceptional pictures.

Elsewhere in this book is information regarding technical

and esthetic techniques dealing with normal to poor available light.

How many pictures should a press photographer take at a single event? And consequently, what should be the capacity of frames per roll of the film in the camera and the films in the photographer's camera bag?

The answers to these questions are as individual to each photographer as are the choices of the positions from which to take a picture, exposure values, and when to snap the shutter. However, though you will have to gauge yourself according to the specific event and your initial interpretation of it as a photographer, there are basic guidelines you can follow.

It is best, first of all, to carry both the conventional-sized short (20-exposure) and long (36-exposure) rolls of film with you. Film is also shot in other lengths, such as 24, 72, and 250 frames. However, if you prefer to buy only one size, make it the short ones.

If you like, you can buy large rolls of bulk film in such lengths as 100 feet and load your own reusable cassettes—at a savings after your initial investment.

There will be some spot-news events that will be over so fast following your arrival that you may only have the opportunity to take a few shots. The film will then have to be developed with most of the strip unused, because newspapers must meet deadlines and you just can't wait around for the next news situation to happen to finish out the roll. Therefore, it is suggested that your camera be loaded with a short length of film.

When you get to a scene you will sometimes have an immediate feeling as to whether you will be shooting a few or many pictures. Take the case of a traffic accident in which a person is being extricated from a car. Usually you will first have the chance to take several shots of an overall scene; then there will be a brief span of time during which the victim is transferred from the car to the ambulance via stretcher—at this point, first aid people and onlookers will probably be blocking your view. As a result, you may only be able to get a few pictures of the victim. Once the victim has been placed in the ambulance and the door closed, there is no picture you can take that would be of value to a newspaper—unless the story is so strong that any picture at all will do.

The opposite situation might be represented by a large fire that is becoming extensive, with more and more fire companies and emergency medical people arriving on the scene. A major news event like this will provide you with a wide choice of views, angles, and varieties of action. This will most certainly allow you to offer an editor a good choice of pictures, thereby increasing your chances of making a sale— possibly of more than one picture. Perhaps you might even find yourself in a position to sell photos to more than one market.

When you first get to such a fire, you may want to switch immediately to a long film roll. If you are not sure about how many pictures you will be taking, shoot one short roll first. Afterward you may decide to shoot more.

I was once at a fire in my area, took pictures, returned home, developed them, and passed by the scene again only to find that the fire had spread. I stopped and took more pictures.

Your own temperament as a photographer will be a determining factor in how many pictures you take at a news happening. Some photographers like to take the time to compose a scene in their viewfinder and wait until an ideal moment arrives before taking a picture. Others, who prefer spontaneity, will shoot more pictures at sudden whimsical moments.

When you are covering a planned event, you will usually find it easier to decide on approximately the number of pictures you might expect to be taking.

Should You Shoot in Color?

Although most newspapers deal primarily with the black-and-white medium, some use color. There are newspapers that have the facilities to publish a color photo and do so on occasion, and certain Sunday newspaper magazine inserts carry color. Color can also be found in some national tabloids as well as in the majority of magazines on the newsstands, including the news weeklies.

Your primary concern, however, should be with black-and-white, which, in itself, requires much study and practice. You should concentrate on black-and-white if you plan to pursue newspaper photography full-time or even for an occasional sale. But if you want to be prepared for potential sales in color, the best way to cover a news event is to take along a second camera body. Whatever lens you choose to use—normal, wide-angle, or telephoto—can be transferred back and forth between camera bodies, and similar scenes can be obtained in both media. It is best, however, to give preference to the action with the camera holding black-and-white film, because that is where the majority of markets lie.

Publications that use color require slide rather than negative film.

As for film speed, ASA 400 should also be your choice for color, for the same reasons applied to black-and-white. Color can also be push-processed, though not as far in rating as black-and-white because of a shift in color value.

If you are shooting an incident in both black-and-white and color, you can take advantage of the two cameras by checking one camera's metering system against the other's. If both cameras are using ASA 400 films, the *f*-openings at identical shutter-speeds should be the same. If you use a film speed of ASA 200 with one film and ASA 400 with the other, the lower rating, being one-half of the other, should require one additional *f*-opening. The subject of film speeds is dealt with in more detail in Chapter 5.

You can develop certain color films yourself. Sometimes newspapers have on hand the necessary chemicals and knowledgeable personnel to use them. There are also custom labs that process some types of color film. Other color films must be developed by the manufacturer, which means a wait of a week or more. So if you put color film into your camera bag, be certain that your choice will not cause you to run into excessive delays in processing.

If you have color pictures of an event that an editor wants, it will be developed on a rush basis at the publication's expense. All you have to do is pick up the phone, find a market, and convince the appropriate individual there that you have a picture they want. If you are offering something very unusual, it won't require much salesmanship on your part, and you will find that transportation of your film will be arranged for you.

Never be afraid to call a publication. Who you are is not important to them—what you have to offer is.

If you have one camera body and want to use it to shoot in both black-and-white and color, you will either have to wait until your roll of black-and-white is finished or rewind the film before it is fully exposed, for later use. If you rewind it before reaching the end, take note of what frame number you have reached. You can write this on the emulsion side of the film leader with a pen or pencil. However, when rewinding the film back into the cassette, be careful that the leader is not drawn completely inside, that it remains free to be started in your camera again in the take-up spool and sprockets. Do this by rewinding it slowly. You will feel an increasing tightness; then, as the beginning of the roll is reached, you will feel the tension let up. Immediately following that, there will be a slight snap as the take-up spool releases the leader. At that point, you can open the camera and remove the film.

When reloading the partially exposed roll, set your camera at its fastest speed and the lens at its smallest opening to avoid double-exposing the used frames. Then, in the shade, cover the lens with your palm and shoot off the number of pictures you have already taken, plus one more, so that your next picture does not overlap the used section.

An important point: don't take color pictures of an accident for your local newspaper, thinking that they can develop them and then convert them to black-and-white. All that work is too much trouble, too time-consuming, or may just be impossible. Only a picture of extraordinary news interest would encourage an editor to endure such an inconvenience—if it is even possible by deadline.

If you are considering using color on occasion, it is best to work with rolls containing the least numbers of exposures.

One snowy, icy day I was given a freelance assignment by a local newspaper to go to a bridge where it was reported that a car had skidded, knocked out a cement piece, and was hanging over the edge. The traffic was tied up because of the weather, and when I got there the car (and driver) had already been removed. So I was only able to get some shots of the open side of the bridge that the car had pushed out. After taking the shots, I went to a nearby phone and called the newspaper to tell them what I had so they would know what to expect me to bring in shortly.

Someone in the store I was in overheard me on the phone and, after I hung up, showed me a 110 pocket camera, saying, "I got pictures of it," and asked, "What will the newspaper pay?"

I called the newspaper back and spoke with the photo editor about the new development. The editor asked me—from experience—"Was it taken in color?"

I asked the person with the camera.

It was color, all right.

And it was no sale.

The newspaper used my picture of the opening in the bridge. Even if they had used a picture from the camera of the person who had been there on the spot, I still would have been paid, since it was an assignment. And that camera might very well have contained an eye-catching photograph.

For press photography, then, always be prepared to use the fastest black-and-white film in the smallest rolls. And be sure you have enough rolls in your camera bag. Although the best photo might be the first one you snap, it may, on the other hand, take several rolls to get that one saleable picture.

Sometimes you will know instinctively the instant that

"perfect" shot appears in your viewfinder. And after you have captured that moment with a movement of your finger, you will have a rewarding feeling of confidence and elation. There is hardly anything like it for a photographer.

Filters

It is a good idea to keep a set of filters in your camera bag. The basic ones are skylight, red, yellow, and green.

A skylight filter serves more than one purpose. Its theoretical use is to cut through haze, which it does. But a practical use for this filter is to protect your lens.

The skylight filter should be kept on your camera at all times. It will not adversely affect your pictures, whether black-and-white or color. At the same time, it will prevent your lens from getting wet from rain, from being damaged by flying debris, and from being broken if it is accidentally bumped.

There is, of course, an abundance of information regarding basic filters that deals with visual enhancement of certain objects of varying colors. General facts follow.

A yellow filter will make clouds more evident on your film than they would be without a filter. It will also heighten the contrast of people, buildings, and other subjects in your scene.

A red filter will provide even more intensive cloud and subject differentiation. It can also simulate night scenes.

A green filter provides enhancement of foliage and landscapes.

An orange filter will be effective for visual drama in marine and mountain scenes.

A polaroid filter—and some may be rotated for specific adjustment—can be used to eliminate glare and reflection.

Although exposures are affected by most filters, which require additional light of about one *f*-stop or more, no adjustment is needed for the skylight filter.

A through-the-lens meter will automatically compensate for a filter, with the result that you will not have to make any calculations.

Be careful about using more than one filter at a time. The rings that hold them might block off the corners of your negative frames.

If you are shooting in color, you may have to use filters for converting daylight film for tungsten lighting and vice versa.

5

Exposure

Exposure is comprised of three factors: film speed, shutter speed, and lens opening (also called aperture, *f*-opening, or *f*-number).

With one of these factors held constant, the remaining two work proportionately with each other. Being that film speed is usually the constant factor, if another factor is doubled, the third should be halved. Regarding aperture, as will be explained, each successive *f*-stop either doubles or halves the amount of light that enters the camera—you do not double or halve the *f*-number itself.

If your exposure determination is based on the film package instructions, you will find only one shutter speed with which to work, and the aperture to be used at that speed under different light conditions. With this information as a basis from which to calculate, however, you can compute the aperture needed for any speed your scene may require. For example, using a popular film speed for press photography—

ASA 400—you might have a recommendation for a bright but slightly overcast (not totally sunny) day of 1/250 second at $f/11$.

Now, suppose you will be shooting an extreme close-up of a fireman holding a hose against a background of many other firemen fighting a blaze. You will need as much depth of field (discussed later) as you can get. To obtain this, you would use the next f-number, $f/16$. However, since $f/16$ would allow half as much light into the camera, you would have to compensate by cutting your speed in half, to 1/125 second. This would allow double the half amount of light in through the lens.

Suppose you want to get even closer to the subject to obtain a tight shot of the badge on his fire hat against the same background. In such a case, even more depth of field would be needed to keep the distance in focus. An exposure of 1/60 second at $f/22$ would no doubt be safe from the blurring of movement since at that speed a fireman holding a hose is likely to be relatively still.

On the other hand, there might be an occasion when you might not want the background in focus. This could be a situation in which you are shooting a subject from extremely close up, behind whom there is too much visual distraction. For example, suppose you are photographing a politician who is standing in front of you on a grandstand—behind whom many other officials are sitting. You want to throw out of focus those vividly sharp faces both to bring attention to your subject and to create an atmosphere of an indistinct crowd. You would, therefore, quickly set your camera to its highest speed, which may be 1/1000 second or even 1/2000 second. On an average overcast day, as the one described earlier, with a film of ASA 400, this would bring your aperture to $f/4.5$ at 1/2000 second by a simply calculated progression.

Beginning with your package insert information, you would adjust your lens to the desired speed and its required aperture for the existing light conditions by moving each over a notch at a time.

To create an example that would best demonstrate this conversion, let's assume that your package insert recommends

1/60 second at $f/22$ for the conditions under which you plan to shoot. You would then convert your aperture for 1/2000 second as follows:

> 1/60 second at $f/22$
> 1/125 second at $f/16$
> 1/250 second at $f/11$
> 1/500 second at $f/8$
> 1/1000 second at $f/5.6$
> 1/2000 second at $f/4.5$

Using a through-the-lens exposure meter this would, of course, be calculated electronically for you. But you should, nevertheless, be aware of the mathematics and mechanics behind this theory. In that way, you will lose little time adjusting your camera following that moment of decision to alter speed and aperture drastically. You will know what the limits are and whether the film will allow you to use the exposure setting you wish, rather than discover that your dials will turn no farther. In addition, you will be prepared to move the speed and f-dials in the proper directions, without losing time guessing which is right. And you will be able to double-check your meter to see if it is operating properly, since it should provide the comparable ratio after adjustment. If it doesn't, your batteries or camera should be checked.

Aperture

Lens openings, designated by f-stops or f-numbers, determine the amount of light that reaches the film. The series of progressions on your camera lens should contain part or all of the following numbers or their approximations: 1 (or 1.2), 1.4 (or 1.8), 2, 2.8, 4 (or 4.5), 5.6 (or 6.3), 8, 11, 16, 22, 32, 64. The numbers in parentheses are essentially variations of the preceding number. Each increment of these numbers, which provides a smaller aperture, allows one-half the amount of light into the camera. Note that alternate numbers (1, 2, 4, 8, 16, 32) are multiples of 2.

Depth of Field

An optical phenomenon related to aperture is depth of field, which concerns the zone in which objects are in focus. For example, if your subject is a person standing ten feet away from you, and you are using a wide lens opening (low *f*-number), the background will be out of focus as will be any object that is five feet from you. With a very small aperture (high *f*-number), the background and foreground objects will be in focus along with your subject.

There are a few ways of determining depth of field. One is by obtaining literature from the manufacturer, if it is available. However, most lenses marketed today have scales on the lens barrel that indicate the zone of focus at each aperture.

Some lenses have a feature by which, after setting your aperture, you can temporarily stop down from the largest opening—through which you are focusing the camera—to that specific opening. This allows you actually to see in your viewfinder what you will or will not get in focus. Other cameras are automatically stopped down when you set your exposure. The only drawback to focusing this way is that the view through the finder is dim.

You can also experiment by taking pictures of objects at various measured distances, then making a record of the results for future reference.

When employed as an artistic device, depth of field is an element of photography that is extremely useful in the taking of press pictures. A person can be featured large against a related scene that is sharply in focus. Or that same photo can be turned into a mood shot simply by using a large aperture to put the same background out of focus.

A shot taken of a line of picketers stretching away from the photographer can have all the words on their signs in focus or out of focus. If the day is overcast, requiring a large aperture, you can compensate for this disadvantage by standing back farther from the group. The depth of field, which increases with distance, is therefore greater. On a sunny day you could use a smaller aperture and stand closer.

In sports photography a telephoto lens must be focused sharply at the distance at which the photographer follows a key player or expects the action to occur. Any person or object just slightly closer or farther than that distance will be out of focus.

A good depth of field in sports photography is an asset: the smaller the lens opening used, the deeper the range of focus available for athletes closer to or farther away from the photographer than the primary subject or subjects. But, at the same time, athletes require a fast shutter speed, which dictates the use of a large aperture. Therefore, compromises must be made.

As mentioned earlier, the shorter the focal length of the lens, the greater the depth of field—even at smaller f-numbers (larger apertures). Therefore, a wide-angle lens—ranging from the fish-eye of approximately 6mm to the commonly used 35mm size—will give you an advantageous depth of field, provided you can get close to your subject. Naturally, in sports a wide-angle lens would be of little use for action shots because it would put your subjects far away, making them too small in relation to your frame. However, if you are featuring a coach or player at the sidelines, to whom you can get close, with the playing field and stands in the background, it would be of benefit.

You should constantly consider the depth of field offered by each of your lenses whenever you are selecting one for a news shot or composing a scene in your viewfinder. Always look to take advantage of an effect that a lens can offer you that might improve your results in some way.

Shutter Speed

Most fixed-speed cameras have shutters that operate at 1/30 second. At this speed, the person taking a photograph must hold the camera very still. It is good practice, in fact, to make a special effort to move only your finger while tripping the shutter in order to avoid movement and resultant blurring.

A good average speed to use for press photography with an adjustable shutter lies in the range of 1/100 to 1/125 second. Sometimes, though, if you expect to be close to a person and there is a chance that there might be more than average movement—such as a speaker waving a demonstrative fist—take the precaution of setting the shutter speed at 1/250 second. If this can't be done in time or isn't possible, at least a blurred fist might create an effective emphasis in the picture.

On the other hand, when photographing a scene that includes virtually no movement—a room in a museum, a house that has burned down, or a relatively motionless group of people, for example—a speed of 1/30 second will allow you to use a small aperture. This results in providing greater definition, or sharpness, and depth of field.

Steady hands are usually enough to hold a camera reasonably motionless for a speed as low as 1/30 second—and sometimes even 1/15 second. However, when shooting at such low speeds, or lower, sharp results can be assured if the photographer and/or the camera are braced.

To hold a 35mm camera firmly, place one hand under the barrel of the lens. This will allow you to adjust aperture while supporting the camera. Hold the side of the camera with the other hand, using a finger to trip the shutter. Press the camera firmly against your face. This will prevent any hand movement that would occur if you were holding the camera free.

For further assurance of camera steadiness, if it is possible to brace your body as well, do so—against a wall, bookcase, or anything else that is stationary and convenient. In some situations you will be able to put your camera on a fixed object such as a table or the back of a chair. If your camera is braced solidly, you might be able to go to a speed as low as one second, which can give you good pictures under extremely poor light conditions.

For two reasons, the use of a telephoto lens requires a higher speed than would normally be used for a regular lens. First of all, closer proximity to your subject requires a faster speed because of relatively faster movement as perceived by the camera. Whereas a slight head movement might not be discernible in a full-length photo of a person, a close-up of the subject's head would undoubtedly show any movement. Second, your own naturally unsteady movements, no matter how slight, are magnified in proportion to the relative degree of closeness to the subject. As a result, a proportionate increase in speed will be necessary.

Suppose you are taking pictures of a virtually motionless scene with a 50mm lens at 1/30 second and wish to change to a 200mm lens. The increased focal length is four times the original. Therefore, your speed should be increased proportionately. This is obtained by dividing the speed, 1/30 second, by four. The result is 1/120 second and its approximate equivalent on your camera is probably about 1/125 second.

A sports shot taken at 1/125 second in the same 50mm to 200mm situation would be increased at the same one-to-four ratio—to 1/500 second.

In both cases, of course, the f-number would be decreased by two stops, which is an increase of four times the light because the speed, doubled twice, would be four times the original shutter speed.

Speed and aperture must always be balanced with respect to what you desire in depth of field. At a news scene, you must immediately decide whether you want the background in or out of focus. Then you will know whether you should put priority on a large or small f-number.

At the same time, however, you will have to work within the bounds of your film speed and the light available—or what illumination you can add with floodlights, flash, or room lights.

Unusually-Lit Scenes

Occasionally, you will be confronted by a scene that will "fool" your camera's exposure meter. You must be aware of such misreadings when they occur, because if you accept this incorrect information as supplied by the electronics of your camera and set your exposure accordingly, you will discover upon development of your film that your negatives are either underexposed or overexposed.

An example at each end of the spectrum would be 1) a beach scene and 2) a stage scene—both taken a good distance away from persons who are subjects of the pictures.

First, let's consider the beach scene. If people are the subjects, they are the part of the picture that should be exposed properly. However, the reflective capacity of sand causes a meter—which judges an overall view, or at least its major area—to appraise the scene generally as being extremely bright, despite the fact that people in the scene reflect less light back to the camera. The subjects, therefore, are not being metered properly by the camera. If the camera were close to the subject, the meter would observe less light coming back and the subject would be correctly exposed. The sand, instead, would be poorly exposed, becoming overly white without detail in the finished picture, which would be no loss. As a result of the misreading, however, the photographer improperly matches up aperture and speed with the result that less light than needed is allowed into the camera. Consequently, the subject is underexposed.

Now, the opposite situation: Taking a reading of a mostly dark stage with faces here and there lit by spots, your exposure meter would ascertain that its field of view is, in general, extremely dark. Therefore, it would indicate that you should adjust to an exposure that would allow more than necessary light into your camera. As a result, your subjects will be overexposed.

In the beach scene, the underexposure would leave no details of your subjects' faces on the negative. Therefore, when printed, the subjects' faces would be dark. The stage scene, by being overexposed, would produce densely dark faces on the negative that, when printed, would be too light, the details of the features being lost.

It is possible, of course, to compensate for such misreadings. First, you must be able to recognize a lighting situation that can deceive your through-the-lens (or hand-held) meter. You will then be able to compensate by making adjustments accordingly. Otherwise, you will discover after the film is developed that you have not taken well-exposed pictures.

Unusually-Lit Subjects

There are some less extreme situations that also require special exposing for the best results. An example might be when the primary subject (close-up) of your shot is a person whose face is in shadow, and the background is sunny. In this situation, if you just aim your camera and adjust it according to its reading, you will "average" the light by metering the scene in general. The result will be that your background will be somewhat bleached out but will retain reasonable detail. Details of the subject's face, though, will be lost because of insufficient exposure. In other words, you will have taken a less than perfectly exposed photo. However, if you expose for your subject's face, it will be properly exposed even though in shadow. The background, which is unimportant, will then be almost totally bleached out.

On the other hand, suppose the situation were reversed—the primary subject in sunlight and everything else in shadow. Then, if the meter reading is followed exactly, the subject might turn out to be overexposed. Again, you should expose for your subject, which would produce an underexposed background.

Exposing for Stark Contrasts

Occasionally you will be confronted with a situation in which people you are photographing, and the area in which they are situated, are adjacent to another area that has totally contrasting lighting. As an example, let's consider a ball game on a field, with players, against a crowded grandstand high above them. Using this situation, here are examples: 1) a sunny field and the stands in shadow; 2) the field in shadow with sun on the stands.

If the field is more important, expose for that, and you will have detail in the field area—with a great loss of detail in the stands. If you expose for the stands, you will have good detail there with lost detail on the field. Should you be shooting one or the other separately, of course, you would have the best exposure results for each.

If you want it all, you will have to take an overall exposure reading. As a result of using this average exposure for the full scene, you will lose some detail in each section, but you will have a picture with values of shading that range evenly in density throughout the entire picture.

Standard Exposure Compensation Techniques and Devices

Up to this point, we have discussed situations in which your through-the-lens meter either cannot give you delicate information regarding a section of your scene that you wish to concentrate on with the exposure, and those in which the meter is drastically incorrect due to extreme contrast in lighting of different areas. In those discussions, we have referred to "exposing for" specific portions of your scene. How do you go about this?

One way to handle exposure meter misreadings— recommended by many photography books and articles—is to adjust your aperture upward or downward by 1, 1½, or 2 f-stops (or change your shutter speed accordingly, which is equivalent). The problem with this method is that it requires guessing or, at least, a great deal of experience—best obtained by practice and comparison studies of results. However, by *bracketing*—shooting with apertures set at, above, and below what you think might properly expose the film—you will be fairly certain to get one correct exposure. In press photography, though, there often isn't time for this kind of hit-and-miss experimentation.

Alternatively, you can choose to change the ASA adjustment

on your camera. But, if you do, be sure to restore the correct setting after your special-case pictures have been taken.

You may wish to invest in a device called a spot meter. This instrument is capable of taking a reading of a limited area. By looking through its viewfinder, you evaluate a small circumscribed portion. This might be the limited region of a scene that is to be photographed with a telephoto lens, or it could be a small area of an overall scene that you wish to expose for especially without regard to the rest of the picture—as with the face in shadow described earlier.

A spot meter can take the light measurement on the face of an actor on stage—from the audience. Thus, if you were using a 200mm lens, for example, to photograph an actor lit by a spotlight, the spot meter would give you a reading of the subject as if you were only inches away—even better than the meter evaluation you would get with the telephoto—allowing you to properly expose your film. As a result, you would be able to obtain delicate values of light and shade on the face and torso. Consequently, the massive dark areas surrounding the actor that would ordinarily confuse a through-the-lens camera meter would not be an obstacle. A camera meter would average out the total light and darkness in your viewfinder, calculating the total amount of illumination to be low, which would require you to give the scene more exposure. And if the majority of the stage is primarily in darkness, a through-the-lens meter might even give you no reading at all.

Nevertheless, using a spot meter requires extra seconds—to take it out of your camera bag or pocket, make adjustments, check its computations, and transfer that information to the settings on your camera.

These methods of correcting camera meter misreadings are effective ways to deal with shooting feature pictures when you have time to plan, when there is no pressure, or when the conditions of an event are not expected to change suddenly. But at a spot-news happening, you have only a moment to set your camera correctly and trip your shutter.

Hints for Expedient Press Photography Metering

I use methods of compensating for meter misreadings that I find fast and effective. Here are some ways I overcome metering situations that can yield underexposed or overexposed photos.

For outdoor scenes, I first decide what area I will be framing by looking through my viewfinder. I then select a limited area within the boundaries of the scene in my viewfinder that I will want best exposed—the center, or perhaps just a face. Next I make a quick eye evaluation of the quantity of light on this subject and whatever I wish to include in the exposure range. Perhaps a subject is in shadow against a light background. Searching for a full viewfinder that seems to average approximately an equivalent amount of light of the area I want perfectly exposed—say, the face alone—I then quickly move my camera toward the ground, crowd, or anywhere else that will give me an equivalent light value. This is, of course, a subjective evaluation, but with practice and constant careful examination of your results, you can develop an ability to match up these values quite closely. When you have a scene with equivalent lighting in your viewfinder, match up your needles or whatever other indicators your camera has for shutter speed and aperture. Then, leaving these settings untouched, get your subject in the viewfinder again. The exposure indicator will then naturally move from the reading that you just set up, perhaps drastically. Ignoring exposure setting now, take the pictures of your major subject at those peak moments of drama—and they will all be correctly exposed.

If you plan to take a close-up of a face against a bright sky, first move in close to the subject and take a reading of the person's face in sunlight or shadow, whichever way you plan to shoot it. Then use that exposure no matter what your meter says when you photograph the subject against the sky. This also applies to full-length shots of your subject for which you would stand back for the initial reading—not against the sky, but in an area lit the same as the subject.

Now for some indoor techniques for light readings that are often misread by a meter. In the theater situation discussed, if you are shooting a school show, local production, or any stage piece for which you are able to check the lighting ahead of time, such as during rehearsals or immediately prior to the show, you can determine your needed exposure by a simple means. Take an exposure reading of an actor from close up with the stage lights on, then make a record of that speed and aperture and use it when you take your pictures from the audience. Despite the dark areas that would give you a false reading from far away when the show is on, you will have an exact exposure. If an actor is not available, use anyone with average reflective clothing—nothing extremely dark or light. At worst, if no one is able to pose for your reading, put one hand in front of the camera under the spotlights where the actor will be. Move your hand at a distance from the lens that will approximate an average mix of light and shadow and take your reading using your other hand to turn the aperture dial.

When I am photographing an object such as a lamp, small statue, or other such piece in a room where there is light from the outside, I place the piece on a table or chair near a window—or more than one window, if possible. The best results are obtained when light is entering from windows on two or more walls from crosslighting. I then move in closely to a representative area of the object, where average light is falling, and take my reading. Then, with the exposure set, I move back to take in the subject in its entirety. The exposure may seem to drop off according to your meter because of the darkness surrounding the object, but ignore this. Naturally, I use the slowest speed I can handle, if I desire a good depth of field.

Aperture Priority

Some sophisticated cameras have a built-in convenience called aperture priority. When the camera is put into this automatic mode, the photographer can set a lens opening and the speed will be varied by electronics so that it complements the chosen aperture for a correct exposure. By using this device, you are freed from having to adjust the camera for the proper exposure. In addition, if the light should change—as the result, for example, of the sun going behind a cloud—the camera will automatically compensate by lowering the speed.

Shutter Priority

Shutter speed priority is also available. When this automatic mode is used, after the camera is set for a specific speed the aperture is automatically changed.

For sports, shutter priority is preferable because the photographer can stay with a selected speed for a specific type of game. However, the photographer must especially beware of exposure meter misreadings with either of these priorities. In instances of misreadings, as previously noted, the camera will take pictures at incorrect exposures. Therefore, when aperture or shutter priority is in operation, the photographer should be certain that the lighting on the scene in the viewfinder averages out as normal to the eye; that is, it should not—as with a beach or stage scene—seem overly bright or overly dark in total.

The Challenge of Photojournalism

As a press photographer, then, you must be able—and prepared—to think and act quickly in order to obtain proper exposures in unpredictable situations. The light at a news or feature scene can sometimes, upon your arrival, be totally different than expected, or it may change or be changed without a moment's notice.

You might discover that the film in your camera is not best suited for the sudden new developments of action or lighting, yet you have only moments to act or you will lose the fleeting chance to capture an important image on your film. In such a case you will have to compromise with speed and aperture, perhaps getting some blurring or a slightly underexposed negative, which can be corrected in the darkroom with a filter or multigrade paper.

But remember, adverse conditions can sometimes give you pictures that have more to offer than what you might ordinarily get under normal, easy-to-work circumstances.

However, it is important that you, as a news photographer, first be resourceful enough to obtain an image on your film, no matter what situation suddenly confronts you.

Although I am not enamored of direct flash to light a scene, there are times when there is no other choice. This is such a situation.

A pedestrian, struck by a car at night, lies in the street. Local first-aiders who arrived quickly at the scene await their ambulance.

6

Flash

There are many ways to use flash other than as ordinary direct illumination by which the flashgun, mounted on the camera, sends out a blast of light parallel to the photographer's line of vision from the viewfinder.

The advantage of direct flash is that it projects its maximum quantity of light on the subject; therefore, you can shoot at reasonably long distances from the subject, depending, of course, on the power of your flash and the ASA rating of your film. The disadvantage is that it results in flat lighting with heavy shadows.

Another kind of flash illumination is called *bounce* flash. This lighting is created by bouncing the flashgun light off a ceiling, wall, or other surface or surfaces. This produces a softer lighting because the light becomes diffused, reaching the subject from many directions, with the result that shadow areas are not totally dark. By the time, though, that the light reaches the subject, its intensity has been attenuated. Consequently, compensation through exposure, film, or developing is required.

Flash is also used for *fill-in*. Suppose you are taking a picture on a sunny day of an official cutting a ribbon, and the sun is behind the subject. In such a situation, it is usually impossible to rearrange the scene. You can, of course, set a shutter speed and aperture that are appropriate for the shadowed area of the subject. However, your results will show an extremely bright halo—one that might eliminate portions of the subject's outline, making it look misshapen. But by using flash fill-in, you can equalize the light. With careful calculation of exposure, in fact, you can even produce a highly pleasing effect with the subject backlighted.

First, let's consider straight flash. Exposure is determined by use of a table of guide numbers provided by the flashgun manufacturer. Merely look up the appropriate number for the film you are using and divide that number by the distance of your camera from the subject; that will give you the *f*-number. For example, if the guide number is 110 and you are ten feet from the subject, you should use $f/11$.

With the use of strobe, the speed of the camera shutter does not affect the results. This is because the speed at which the picture is taken is determined by the speed of the flashgun light. However, shutter speeds are critical in cameras using flashbulbs, which open their shutters as the bulb reaches a peak of brightness.

Strobe flash is extremely fast. Therefore, though your shutter may be set for 1/100 second, you may be taking a picture at anywhere between 1/1000 and 1/30,000 second. As a result, despite the limitations of your maximum shutter speed, you can obtain excellent stop-action for sports when strobe is your only means of light.

Some cameras are designed for the use of both flashbulbs and strobe.

If your camera has a focal plane shutter—as opposed to a leaf (iris) shutter—there is a shutter speed above which you must not set your camera. This is because strobe does not, like a flashbulb, slowly build to a peak and then drop off. As a result, light is reflected back to the camera quickly; subsequently, a fast-moving focal-plane slit does not allow the entire negative area to receive all the light. Many focal plane cameras have built-in features for avoiding the use of improper high speed for strobe.

When using strobe flash, then, always be certain your shutter speed is correctly set at the limit or below; otherwise, you will not get your pictures. The shutter-speed limit, usually in the 1/100 to 1/125 second range, is provided in the camera instructions and often noted in color on the dial which sets the speed.

When using bounce flash, a number of factors must be taken into consideration for determination of exposure as well as for the balance of light and shadow on your subject. First of all, you must consider how many surfaces from which you will be reflecting your light. If the flash is angled so that it will give multiple reflections from the ceiling and walls, it will in a sense be equivalent to studio light using several spotlights. This will result in attractive complex light and dark areas, none heavily shadowed.

Various types of diffusers are available to soften shadowing. These cover the bare flashbulb or reflect its light. A handkerchief, a white card, or any similar device can be used.

Some flashguns, while still attached to the camera, can be angled away from the subject for the bouncing of light. Removal of the flashgun from the camera, while the flash is still operative by wire, can provide additional reflective versatility.

Off-the-camera use of the flashgun, aimed directly at the subject from high above and to the side of the camera, gives longer, more effective shadowing to facial features. It also throws shadows of people's heads low rather than directly behind them. This avoids black halos that detract from the quality of such photos when published in the newspaper, in which dark tones of heads and shadows often merge.

When using this off-the-camera technique of direct flash, be certain that your flashgun is properly aimed; otherwise, the light will be uneven.

If you are bouncing the light off a ceiling to light a person, aiming the flash at a point on the ceiling between you and the subject will produce heavier shadows under the subject's eyes than would be achieved if the flash were aimed at the ceiling behind you. However, the latter variation of bounce lighting will illuminate the subject less, requiring a larger aperture or other compensation. This is illustrated by calculation of your exposure: in bounce flash, you must consider the entire distance from flashgun to subject. This means that you must determine the distance from the flash to the surface off which you are bouncing it, plus the continued distance to your subject. So, though you may be standing only eight feet from your subject, the distance that the light is traveling via the ceiling may be twenty feet. Therefore, you should divide your guide number by twenty—but only if the ceiling is a light color, preferably white.

Should the ceiling be dark, less light will be reflected, and you will have to use your intuition and experience to determine whether you should open your aperture one, two, or more f-stops than your calculation suggests. Very dark reflecting surfaces can leave you with no pictures. So, if you have only distant or poor reflecting surfaces with which to work, it is best that you use direct flash.

Flashguns that incorporate thyristor circuits usually take the guesswork out of bounce flash. After you set your aperture and flash controls according to the directions, a sensitive component of this system takes a reading of the subject during the instant of exposure and cuts the light off when enough has been used to give you a perfect exposure. It also allows you to test your equipment on the scene before you take the picture so that you can tell whether a flash picture is possible under those specific conditoins.

But thyristors can be fooled by above- or below-average reflectance from a subject. For example, a person standing in a large dark space—perhaps in an open wooded area at night, far from the camera—will cause this flash system to read much less light than it should to light the subject properly and will consequently send out too much extra illumination. On the other hand, high reflectance—as, for instance, by a large white sheet on which a baby is being photographed—will make the thyristor sensing device think that the scene is bright, with the result that the amount of flash provided will underexpose the film.

Therefore, when photographing scenes of other than average reflectance, for best results determine your exposure by the distance factor and flash guide number.

Multiple flash may also be used. This is accomplished either by wiring two or more flashguns together or by using one or more *slaves*. A slave is a device that is attached to a wireless flashgun. The instant that it perceives the burst of a flash, it triggers its own flashgun.

For multiple flash use the same exposure as you would for one flash or let your thyristor system help you determine the exposure. However, since light quantities and shutter responsiveness may be a complex matter in multiple flash, experimentation may be necessary.

Flash can also be controlled by radio devices attached to the camera that set off remote lights.

Exposure for flash fill-in is determined after first deciding whether you wish the existing light to appear to be strong or weak in your photograph. It is also possible to deliver a specific quantity of light to a subject so that windows in the background are lit equivalently, giving the photograph depth. The methods for calculating fill-in flash are explained in Chapter 7.

Most flashguns illuminate the field in the camera's view as taken with a "normal" lens (for a 35mm camera, a focal length of about 50mm). If the photographer uses a wide-angle lens, only the center area is properly lit, the light dropping off at the edges. However, flashguns are available that either incorporate or accept their own special wide-angle lenses for a broad projection of light. Similarly, these flashguns also have lenses for complementary use with telephoto lenses—for concentration of light.

If you wish to use a wide-angle lens indoors and either do

not have the time to set up for it or do not have a flashgun that provides wide-angle light, you can widen it yourself by bouncing the light from a standard flashgun off a ceiling or other nearby surface.

Flash, then, can range from crude and brutal to delicate use, depending on bare necessity under the pressure of time to less demanding circumstances that allow meticulous planning. The press photographer—when there is time for extensive contemplation or even when a decision must be made immediately—must always consider what end product is desired. Producing a photograph that engraves well for a newspaper, with a wide range of gray nuances ranging between white and black, is always the goal of the concerned photojournalist.

When the light at a scene cannot provide a subtle range of tones, it is up to the newspaper photographer to supplement it, to provide the editor with the best photograph possible under those adverse conditions.

7

Available Light Techniques

Available light in photography usually refers to light conditions under which "normal" exposures cannot be used. It can be illumination produced by natural or artificial light or both.

A subject lit by direct sunlight or reflected sunlight coming through a window is being lit by available light, as opposed to being lit outside under the same source of illumination.

Outside, a simple meter reading of the subject or subject area can be taken and the exposure set. But when the same person is illuminated inside by the same light coming through the window, other factors must be taken into consideration:

How well is the subject being lit in total?

How much natural light surrounds the subject?

Is there any artificial light on the subject from the inside?

If so, how much light is there as compared to the exterior light?

Is additional light reflected from the interior walls or other surfaces?

Can reflection of the available light be made on the subject through artificial means?

Are there any lamps or other lights that can be turned on to add light to the subject?

Can floodlights or flash be used to fill in dark areas?

Do you want to create an effect of extreme light and shadow contrasts?

Do you want to expose for the subject's shadowed face and let the bright available light highlight that person from behind?

Would you prefer a silhouetted subject?

All these points, and more, must be considered with regard to the way you would like to have the subject and/or scene lit in your finished photograph. Once the lighting conditions are evaluated and your decisions are made, you must then consider whether these goals can be accomplished with the film and developer used for normal exposures.

If the subject and area you are photographing are reasonably bright, and the film you are using is relatively fast, you will be able to take your pictures successfully without any modifications. However, if your camera exposure meter shows little or no response to the light available for your picture taking, you will have to consider alternative techniques to achieve the same goals. You will either have to use a faster film or, if what you are using is the fastest in its ASA rating, it may be necessary to employ push-processing in the darkroom.

If you can provide sufficient artificial light through lamps, chandeliers, other sources available at the scene, or through use of spotlights or flash, push-processing may not be necessary. But push-processing is not an aspect of photography that

On assignment for a local newspaper, I was sent to a talmudical institution to photograph Senator Henry M. Jackson, who was a guest speaker.

Since the room was lit by a good number of fluorescent ceiling lights, I decided that, rather than use flash for a conventional frontal shot, I would hike up the ASA rating of the fast film I was using. I then push-processed it in a developer manufactured specifically for that purpose that produces a fine-grain emulsion.

As a result of using a high ASA rating, the audience would also be lit (as it would not be with flash), so I slipped behind the lectern and waited for my subject to turn toward the side of the audience that would allow me to photograph his face.

The resulting lighting with this technique is dramatic not only on the speaker, but on the audience as well.

should be avoided. It can produce highly unusual and artistic special effects that you might otherwise never obtain.

Push-processing is accomplished through modification of developing times and temperatures with developers used for normal development or through use of special fine-grain developers specifically formulated to increase the ASA rating of your film.

To obtain information about the chemicals available for push-processing, just inquire at your local camera store. You should be able to obtain these special chemicals or have them ordered for you. Directions for their use are included in the packages.

However, if you plan to use normal or regular chemicals to push-process, your camera store dealer may not necessarily be familiar with the exact temperatures and time necessary to increase the ASA ratings to your desired speeds. But there are several ways that you can obtain this information, which varies according to the results desired. A number of books are on the market that deal specifically with this topic. Your local camera store might have one or more in its book rack. Or your local library may have some on its shelf or be willing to order them for you.

The customer relations departments of film and photographic chemical companies are always pleased to help their buyers and will be glad to answer your questions by mail and even by phone. In some instances, when certain inquiries are made frequently about specific use of a product, literature may already have been prepared on the subject, ready to send out on request.

A phone call to a local newspaper of reasonable circulation, which would have need for special darkroom developing techniques, might put you in touch with a photographer or darkroom technician who could answer your questions. Perhaps you might phone a regional bureau of a large newspaper or wire service.

A letter or phone call to the staff of a photography magazine should bring you helpful information, since these people are extremely knowledgeable about film processing and it is their job to inform the public about such facts. It has been my own personal experience that they are delighted to aid photographers by providing data that they have obtained through their own experience.

More and more colleges are offering courses in photography, and instructors are always pleased to make suggestions to nonstudents regarding such problems.

There is undoubtedly a photography club in your area— probably more than one. There you should be able to find members who are knowledgeable about push-processing or who have experimented with it.

Whenever you encounter a setting, then, that is ill lit, before you decide to go to the trouble of adding light that is not natural to it, always consider the possibility of using a higher ASA than that at which your film is normally rated. You may, as a result, achieve exceptional—possibly even spectacular— effects, especially if the available light falls interestingly on the subject and background.

I, personally, use direct flash only as a last resort, because of its flat lighting and heavy shadows.

In available-light shooting, especially, the photographer must, in many cases, use the very subjective and nonscientific method of eye evaluation to judge the light values for a subject and scene. This is done through comparison of planes of light; for example, the light intensity of a forehead versus that of a cheek. The dimmer the light, and the more highly rated the film's ASA, the more attention you must concentrate on the judgment, because the problem becomes magnified. But an ability to assess light quantities, if it is not intuitive, can be acquired through the experience of taking pictures under inadequate illumination and carefully examining and evaluating the results.

Now, let's consider various available light situations and how they can be handled. In this discussion, natural light will refer to sunlight, moonlight, or either of these light sources reflected. Artificial light will be considered to be that produced by electricity in such devices as lamps, chandeliers, spotlights, and flash.

Natural Light

Outdoors, when a subject's face is lit along the side by direct sunlight, the areas that are shadowed still receive a reasonable amount of light from the balance of the sky's hemisphere as well as from light reflected by the ground, building facades, and other surfaces.

Indoors, direct sunlight can result in such high contrast that areas that are lit poorly have no tone whatsoever, and results can be blotchy and hardly identifiable.

Outdoors, hazy sun can provide even light on all surfaces of a subject's face. Inside, the same light coming through one window will usually illuminate a subject's face better than direct sunlight, yet shadowed areas may still be below a level that can be recorded on film when the camera is set to expose the lit area properly.

However, in the indoor situation, the photographer can easily take a high-contrast picture. Or, if a range of grays is desired, it can be produced by moving the subject toward the window and the lens closer to the subject. This will light more of the subject's surface area and make a meter reading easier. As a result, a more normally lit photograph—as opposed to one with severe lighting contrast—will result.

The best way for a photographer, remote from the window, to take a picture of a subject rimmed by light, is to move the camera in for a meter reading. This is done close up—at the part of the face receiving the full light, with the window behind the camera. After the exposure is set, the photographer moves back to the original picture-taking position. The meter then, of course, indicates a proportionate drop in light. The photographer ignores this, leaving the meter set as it was in the close-up reading. As a result, the finished picture will show correct exposure of the lit portion of the subject; the shadowed area will properly register slightly or not at all on the film. Otherwise, if the light is averaged from a distance by the meter, the overall scene will be generally overexposed.

By maneuvering a subject near white reflective walls, or by using movable reflective surfaces, additional illumination can be created that will fill in shadowed areas.

Always avoid including a window in your viewfinder when using the exposure meter if its light is overwhelming in comparison to the light on the subject or field of view; it will produce an erroneous reading.

If you are photographing a subject by the light of more than one window, the lighting can become much more interesting. You might want to position the person you are photographing where the light from one window is considerably different in intensity than the other(s) in order to produce studiolike lighting. Light from one window or more that is evenly distributed will allow you to take a general reading of the subject and/or surrounding field.

When working under low light conditions, you must be extremely concerned about the film ASA rating, the shutter speed, the type of developing planned—and the depth of field, which will be determined by these factors.

Each doubling of the ASA rating (for push-processing) at a constant shutter speed increases your f-number by one stop, thereby closing your aperture and increasing your depth of field. For example, an ASA rating of 100 increased to 200 would allow a one-stop change; to 400, another. Raising the rating from 400 to 3200 increases the f-number by three stops (800 = one stop, 1600 = two stops, 3200 = three stops). Halving your shutter speeds further increases your f-stops, because double the quantity of light is allowed to strike the film. As a result, by adjusting ASA rating and shutter speed, you can provide a considerable increase in depth of field.

However, an increase in ASA rating and/or a lessening of shutter speed is not always possible. So it is a good idea—if you are doing interior assignments regularly—to bring with you an assortment of floodlights, reflectors, and photoflood bulbs. These are relatively inexpensive lamps that consist of a bowllike reflector and a clamp that can be squeezed to attach it to a chair or other support. Light stands, if not too inconvenient to transport, could also be taken along.

This light can be used to fill shadow areas. Again, use your eye to judge relative intensity of light in different planes of your subject and scene. By moving your photoflood lamps toward or away from your subject, you can control the nuances of grays, from black to white, that will result in your finished picture.

To obtain a meter reading of the subject with the supplementary use of floods, use the same basic methods you would use outdoors, either by reading the overall scene or by measuring the light on the subject up close. However, be certain that no bare bulbs appear in your viewfinder to throw off the meter measurement of the light intensity of the scene.

Should you wish to silhouette a person—for example, against a stained-glass window—take as close up a reading of the window or bank of windows as possible and expose for that. The windows will show their designs at the correct density; the subject will automatically be silhouetted.

Artificial Light

Basically, artificial light can be utilized in the same way as natural light. Usually, though, it is not as bright as natural light and emanates from more than a single direction, often from several sources. Therefore, it appears flatter and less dramatic than natural light. Whereas intense light can come through a window and highlight a subject, a room light might only provide functional illumination. However, by taking different positions in a room, the photographer can often find angles from which highlights on a subject can be achieved that might duplicate certain studio effects. Experimentally maneuvering a person who is the subject of a photo into different areas and positions can often result in unusual lighting. This, of course, requires of the photographer a keen, observant eye for distinguishing slight differences in light values on the planes of the face as well as the comparative values in the lighting fabric of the background. But it can be done well if the photographer is extremely alert and critical.

Natural and Artificial Light

As long as you are using black-and-white film, you can mix natural and artificial light without problems because there is no need to be concerned about their difference in Kelvin temperatures, which is critical only in the use of color. If you are shooting color, you will have to take into account whether you should use daylight or tungsten film, special filters, or other means for properly balancing hues. All that the photographer working in the black-and-white medium must do is evaluate comparative light intensities.

Often, the photojournalist will be photographing an interior scene that is lit interestingly by exterior light, such as by that coming through a window, and will have an opportunity to supplement this illumination merely by switching on whatever lights are available in the room. The lower the natural light, the more impact such available artificial light can have on the overall results. A photographer's desired effect can be accomplished by setting the exposure for light intensity anywhere between the limits of both extremes.

Flash Fill-In

If a subject is lit partially by natural light—outdoors or indoors—and you would like to fill in the shadow areas with flash, it can be accomplished several ways.

First of all, you can use direct flash. Suppose you are photographing a person who is lit peripherally by strong sunlight. You can simply use the distance factor method—dividing your distance, in feet from the subject, into the guide number as provided for your film by the flashgun manufacturer. This will give you a picture with your subject brightly outlined.

If you have the same situation indoors, with the bright light pouring through the window, you can use the same method and calculations. In addition, though, you also have the option of using bounce flash, which is calculated in the same way as previously described—using the total distance of the light from the flashgun to the reflecting surface to the subject. And you also must take into consideration such factors as dark reflecting surfaces, which can diminish your light, as explained earlier.

Should you wish to provide just about the same amount of fill-in light as is occurring naturally so that there is no heavy highlighting, take an exposure reading from the direction of the window. In other words, take a close reading of the side of the subject's face with the full natural light on it. Then, in order to fill in the shadow area with an equivalent amount of light, make a calculation that gives the distance to stand from the subject so that your particular flashgun lights the field at the proper intensity to achieve your desired results. Here is an example:

The side of the face of your subject, standing next to a window, is lit by diffused light from the sky. When you stand with your back to the window and take a close-up meter evaluation of the subject's cheek, the through-the-lens meter gives you an exposure of 1/60 second at $f/16$.

Go into the interior of the room. The subject, turning to face you, is now lit along one side and dark in front.

Let's assume that your strobe flash guide number is 240. Divide the guide number by the f-number that you just obtained. This (240 ÷ 16 = 15) gives you a distance of fifteen feet. So you stand fifteen feet from your subject, use direct flash, and record both natural and flash light at the same exposure.

There are a number of methods for increasing or decreasing the difference in intensities of natural and fill-in light. In the example given, you can make the resultant peripheral window light more intense or dimmer in your finished print by moving either closer or farther away from your subject and recalculating your f-opening to above or below 16.

Sometimes it might be necessary to reduce the amount of flashgun light because the distance at which you are kept from the subject after calculation, due to its brightness, is disadvantageous. If you need a close-up shot, a zoom lens helps because you can move your camera's view in close without changing your distance.

However, there are a number of ways to adjust the quantity of light striking the subject from your flash when filling in shadows that will allow you flexibility in choosing the distance from your subject. You can bounce the light off the ceiling or other surface. A diffuser, or a cloth or handkerchief, that covers the flash, will cut down the light. Some flashguns incorporate devices that reduce the amount of electricity used; these are adjustable by f-stop units.

These methods of altering the quantity of flashgun light can be employed to put more stress on the available light by making it either greater or lesser than fill-in.

A great deal of depth can be obtained in a picture by photographing a subject by a window and lighting the interior so that its exposure matches that of the outside. In that way, in the finished picture the scenery or activity outside can be seen clearly. To do this, first aim the camera outside, through the window. Take an exposure reading and divide the aperture number obtained into the flash guide number—as explained previously—to determine the distance you should stand from your subject.

When using natural exterior light for highlighting and flash as your main source, you can increase or lessen the intensity of available light to create a desired effect by adjusting your speed or f-opening upward or downward. This does not affect the exposure of the light from the flash, which will always remain the same. It will only increase or decrease the amount of available light striking the film. However, if you have a focal plane shutter, be certain not to set the speed above the limit for flash.

In summary, then, the photojournalist must quickly evaluate the light available at a dim or partially lit scene to determine whether normal film and developing will be sufficient to capture the desired views properly. This is done simply by using the camera meter to measure as many aspects of the setting as possible. If the light is low, yet it is still possible for the press photographer to work with a wide aperture and slow shutter speed, and depth of field is of little importance in the situation, normal exposure and developing will be sufficient. But if, despite the use of a film with a high ASA rating, the light is too low, or more depth of field is desired, the only choices that the photographer has are to use push-processing or flash.

Depending on the quality of available light and the geometry of the setting, the photojournalist must envision the results of each possible approach, evaluate how push-processing or flash would appear in print in the newspaper, decide which direction to take, then make images with that technique a reality on film.

8

Negatives, Clippings, Facts— and Filing

Negatives should be cut into segments and stored in negative envelopes, or glassines, obtainable where photo supplies are sold.

Strips of thirty-six exposures are usually cut into six sections of six frames each. Rolls of twenty exposures can be cut into four strips of five exposures. The number of frames on a strip should be determined by your own method of filing and requirement for storage container size. Some editors cut them into threes.

There are two ways of permanently noting which pictures you have selected. Both are used by newspapers. On the contact proofsheet, chosen frames can be circled with any color of china marker, other crayon, pen, or the like that will write on photographic paper. On the negative strip itself, a paper hole puncher—the kind with a handle—or a scissors, can be used to nick the sprocketed edge (top or bottom) of the frame to be printed. This is an expedient method because in

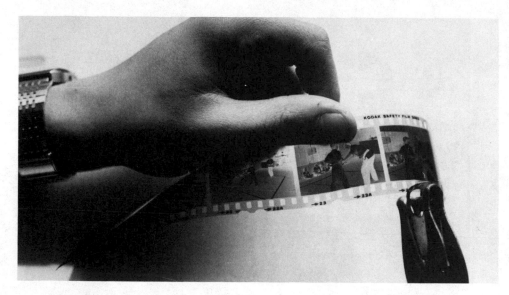

Newspapers usually mark their negative frame choices with a hand paper hole puncher for quick and easy identification in the darkroom. Two nicks means "cancel."

the darkroom it is then necessary only to run a finger along the edge of the negative strip to find the frame selected for printing. Double punching of negatives is also used by editors to cancel a choice.

A 9-x-12-inch manila envelope is handy for filing your work away in a letter file for quick access at a later date. I seal an empty envelope, then cut a thin strip off the top edge, making a container for the negatives, proofs, and discarded or unused prints. In addition, I add my notes of the event or assignment to this material. I also include any newspaper clippings or other material that might be of use later, should I plan to spin off photos or an illustrated article for a magazine or other publication. The date and event are noted on the envelope, as well as on the negative glassines. Material from more than one happening can be filed in the same envelope to save space and expense.

I use a 9- × 12-inch manila envelope, open at the top—each for one or more incidents—to store my negatives, proofs, and notes.

If the negatives are kept by the newspaper, it is still a good idea—for later reference—to write the date and news event on an envelope and file away any related material in it, such as expenses for your assignment.

9

Film Processing

You Don't Need a Darkroom

Starting out in photojournalism, you may be able to put off having to set up a darkroom. It all depends, of course, on the interest and cooperation of the newspapers in your area—and what you bring them in the way of interesting shots.

Sometimes, a newspaper will develop your film. If this is not the case where you live, you can develop your film professionally without a darkroom and offer the actual results of your picture taking—in the negative stage—for immediate examination. To do this, as will be explained, inexpensive basic equipment and supplies are all that are needed, and processing can be done in a kitchen or bathroom.

For temporary darkroom use, public darkroom facilities are available in some areas for rental by the hour. Ask about this at your local camera store or at nearby photography schools.

Area camera clubs also might be helpful. Members often use facilities set up at adult schools, community colleges, or other local institutions and sometimes allow the use of their own personal darkrooms to other members.

When the Newspaper Will Develop Your Film

Most large city newspapers will probably process your film if it seems that you have what they want. A newsworthy incident that sounds, by your verbal description on the phone, like your pictures of it will be eye-catching should interest an editor, especially if the newspaper's photography staff missed it.

If the newspaper is fairly large, but not necessarily a high-circulation publication, there may be no personnel available to develop the film after hours. So, even though there may be someone in the office who is authorized to make a photo purchase, your efforts might be wasted.

It is relatively inexpensive to buy equipment and chemicals just to develop your black-and-white film—without proof or printing or the need for a darkroom. All you need is a tank, thermometer, film reel, and two chemicals mixed and ready to be used.

Being able to show an editor a negative can increase your chances of selling. For one thing, it shows that you know what you are doing—you have the evidence in hand. It could, in fact, be the deciding factor. A good shot speaks for itself.

To take your negatives one step further, you could make a proof. This can be done with a little more investment, using a piece of glass, printing paper, safe light, one more chemical, and a few trays (which could be improvised). With this, you could present an editor with a proof of positive picture frames, and still no darkroom would be necessary.

With one more step up—having an enlarger (and this can be a used or inexpensive one)—you can actually deliver a finished print to the newspaper office. Such prints can be made in a temporary take-down bathroom darkroom. This way, an on-the-spot decision can be made to purchase your picture, and that very photograph that you show to the editor might be the one used for engraving.

You may want to start off by offering only undeveloped film to your local paper to see what response you will get. Perhaps you may want to follow processing partially through, or to the completed, engravable picture. If you are not familiar with the procedure of processing black-and-white pictures, the narrative guide below will take you step by step through each phase of black-and-white photofinishing. If you follow these instructions, your results will be professional. After reading about these developing procedures, you can decide how far you would like to go in processing your pictures.

Developing the Film Yourself—Negatives Only

Apparatus and Supplies

You can purchase basic equipment and chemicals inexpensively in a camera store or in most department store photography departments. An inquiry about prices in your locality will give you an idea of whether you will want to pursue this approach. The most commonly used film for press photography is 35mm. For that reason, the instructions below will deal with that format or size. If you use another format, all that will be different will be the size of your tank and reel or possibly just the reel. The developing procedure will be the same as for 35mm.

Tanks are available that will hold one or more reels.

You will need a darkroom thermometer.

The chemicals that you will require are a film developer and hypo (fixer). You can use stop bath—an intermediate chemical—but it is not essential. If you wish to use stop bath, it can be made easily and cheaply with vinegar and water; stop bath is a weak solution of acetic acid—which is actually vinegar. You can even replace this step by using tap water as a wash.

For measuring your chemicals, an ordinary measuring cup will do. One 35mm roll of film requires exactly eight ounces of each fluid.

Choice of specific brands of chemicals varies with the individual photographer. Any good, established brand will give you excellent results. All you have to do is follow the manufacturer's instructions in the package insert.

For more details on these basics of film developing, you can write to the manufacturer for additional literature, consult a camera store salesman, or check with your local library.

Most importantly, it is best to use a high-contrast developer, because contrast is essential for newspaper photoengravings. When a picture is screened into dots for newsprint, details become lost and the sharp contrast of blacks and whites becomes essential. Flat, gray pictures often become muddy when printed. Fine-grain developers produce a range of grays that not all newspapers can handle in printing.

Loading Film into the Developing Tank

To load the film, use a darkroom or closet. Make certain there are no light leaks. This is easy to check. Go into the room, put out the lights, and wait a minute or so until the pupils of your eyes adjust to the surroundings. If you have any light leaks, you will spot them immediately.

Any stray light, no matter how little, is capable of fogging film. And the longer the light affects the film, as when you have difficulty loading it onto the reel and lose time, the less contrast your final print will have from the graying negative.

If you do have light problems, put a blanket over your hands in the darkroom, or have someone outside the room (which, ideally, should be windowless) hold a blanket up over the light cracks—the location of which you can describe from the inside.

Although it isn't necessary, you could buy a changing bag; this would give you the convenience of not having to use a darkroom at all. A changing bag zips open for putting in the tank, reel, scissors, and a tool for opening the film magazine. It has two light-tight sleeves for your arms. Although there may be light outside the bag, your hands are working in pitch-black darkness inside.

As long as the film is still in the magazine, it can be attached to the developing reel in the light—provided the film leader was not wound into the magazine after the pictures were taken. You can only wind your film after taking pictures so that the leader is out if you have experience based on repeated practice by feel. If you are unable to do this, the beginning of the roll can be retrieved from inside the magazine. A piece of film—or thin, stiff cardboard or plastic—with double-sided tape stuck onto it, should be pushed into the magazine slit where the film once emerged, with the sticky side facing the core. With several turns of the spool, the tape will stick to the film leader, which can then be pulled out. Devices designed specifically to perform this function are available at many camera stores.

If you are unable to retrieve the leader from the magazine, you will have to hook it into the reel in the dark. This may be somewhat more difficult and time-consuming than doing it in the light.

Winding the film into the reel is an important step in the developing procedure. If it is not loaded correctly, it can stick together in spots, resulting in the loss of pictures because the surfaces in contact will not be washed over by the chemicals. By attaching the leader of your film in the light, you can see that it is properly started.

Once the film is caught into the center of the reel, in the dark pull a few inches more film out of the magazine and start it off into the grooves of the reel. Be certain that the film is set properly between the top and bottom of the reel or it may kink and jam; it may even pull loose. If you hooked it into the reel in the light and it gets free—and you either cannot get it back into the magazine, or you have opened the magazine—you will have to start all over again in the dark, hooking it back into the center-of-the-reel catch.

The direction of curvature of the film follows the curvature of the reel.

You can draw the film out of the magazine as you load, but it is easier if you open one end of the magazine and take out the spool of film. The magazine ends can be pried loose with a bottle cap opener. There are, of course, conveniently made tools available for just this purpose.

LOADING YOUR TANK

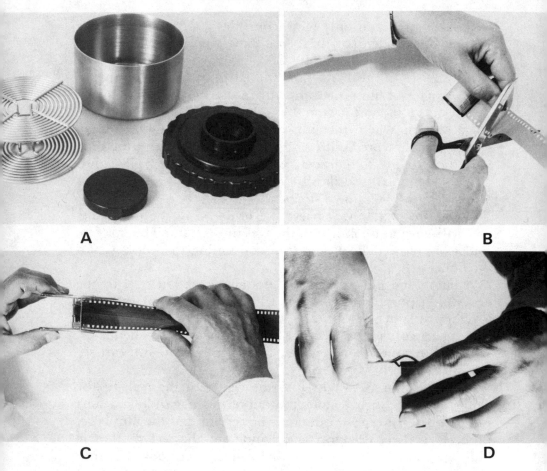

A

B

C

D

A tank and reel for developing one roll of 35mm film of 20 or 36 exposures (A).

If the leader is not rolled into the film magazine after exposure, or if it is retrieved, it can be cut off in the light. Otherwise, this must be done in darkness (B).

Hook the film firmly into the center of the reel. If the previous step has been done in the light, this one can, too (C).

A can opener may be used to remove either side of the film magazine (D).

LOADING YOUR TANK (Continued)

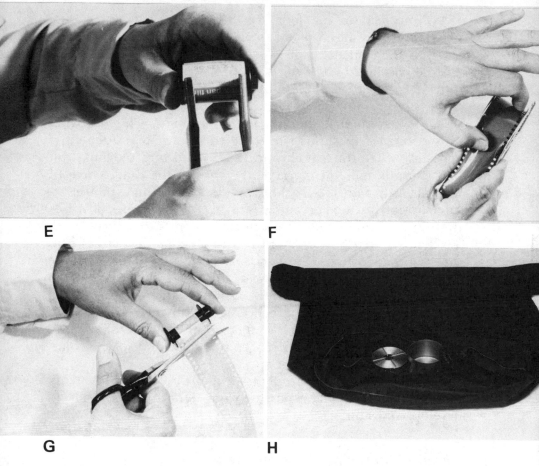

E

F

G

H

Special tools are available for easier removal of the magazine ends (E).

Kinking of film can ruin your negatives during development. By running your thumb and forefinger around the film at each wind, you can detect imperfect curvature and redo that part (F).

Scissors easily detach the film from the spool. It can be torn; however, fingerprints and scratching must be avoided (G).

You can load your tank without worry of light leakage around doors or windows if you use a changing bag (H).

As you reel up the film, touch its surface with as little pressure as possible to avoid leaving marks. The inner surface, which is the emulsion side, is most susceptible to damage.

Hold the film by the edges, curving it slightly to make the inner part concave. This will allow the sprocketed edges to slip easily into the reel grooves.

To be certain that the film is not kinking, which is what causes some of its surfaces to come in contact with each other and stick when the first chemical is poured into the tank, run your thumb and forefinger gently around the outer curve of film at each turn. If the film has buckled, you will feel an interruption in the curvature; pull five or six inches of it free from the reel and wind it back until it is smoothly curved.

When you reach the end of the film where tape attaches it to the spool, cut it loose with scissors or tear it gently from the tape. You can also, instead, tear the tape or pull it off the spool. Wind the final part of the film onto the reel carefully so that it forms a smooth arc concentric with the roll. The very end of the film roll will lean against the surface of the film below it. This is all right; it will not stick. But make certain that the sticky tape has been removed.

Put the reel of film into the tank and the lid onto the tank. The tank can now be exposed to the light. You are ready to develop your film.

Chemicals in General Photography

Many brands of darkroom chemicals for basic use are on the market. In addition, chemicals for more sophisticated purposes are available. Some, for example, are for mixing special formulations of basic chemicals. Others are additives for the enhancement of commonly used solutions. Still others are used for achieving out-of-the-ordinary effects, as with sepia toning of prints and positive reversal.

Chemicals in Press Photography

The press photographer usually prefers to work with film

developers of high contrast. In addition, newspaper photography usually requires that these chemicals perform their functions quickly. When deadlines constantly loom, time is of the essence.

The temperature usually recommended for developing is 68° F. However, package insert instructions commonly provide information about times and temperatures ranging from approximately 65° F. to 75° F. With an increase in temperature, developing time becomes shorter, but there is an increase in graininess. A shorter developing time also brings about a risk of uneven development, because the flow of developer around the entire film strip is less uniform than it is during a longer period. I personally prefer using the lowest allowable temperature, which is most often 65° F. But, when pressed for time, I have had to go as high as 75° for push-processing.

Photographic chemicals for film processing are sold in packages ranging from exact quantities for developing one roll of film to much larger quantities. The purchase of large packages provides excellent savings, but you must consider the shelf life of the mixed solutions, which become less stable with time, in relation to your needs.

Chemicals that are sold in liquid form are usually packed in such a manner as to protect stability for long periods of time. However, premixed liquids are, in general, more expensive than those sold in powder form.

Although manufacturers do not usually recommend mixing proportionate quantities of large units of chemicals, it can in many cases be done when the strengths of the resultant solutions are not critical.

To develop your negatives, it is necessary to have a darkroom thermometer. One used for black-and-white developing is not expensive. Color requires a more expensive thermometer if you want to stay within a range of ½ degree.

It is best to have your solutions already mixed and ready for news events. Otherwise, if you mix them as needed, powders requiring water of high temperature for dissolving will have to be cooled, resulting in the loss of valuable time.

Only the developer requires critical temperature control.

Stop bath and hypo (or fixer) and your water for washing only have to be cool.

Do not use extremely warm, or hot, solutions, which can reticulate your film. Heat can shrivel the emulsion. If extremely hot, it can also cause the emulsion to wash off its strip base. Therefore, while washing negatives check your tap water to be certain that you have not accidentally turned on the hot water.

When you are ready to develop film, there are a number of ways to cool your solution from room temperature, which is about 80° F. If you are mixing a quantity of stock solution—an intermediate liquid between a concentrate or powder and a usable fluid—to which water must be added, running the cold water for a while before dilution will sometimes be effective. Otherwise, you can add an ice cube to the stock solution, stir until the thermometer reads slightly below the desired temperature, then remove the cube and add enough tap water to bring the total up to the required amount. Then, warm or hot water can be run on the outside of the container until the temperature of the solution is correct.

An ice water bath is a way to bring temperature down when your chemical solution cannot be diluted. You can prepare this by putting cold water and ice cubes into a large basin, bowl, or other container. Put your developing solution into a smaller container, preferably of metal—which quickly conducts heat out of the container—and swirl it while the thermometer displays the diminishing temperature.

Another way to cool a solution—without water baths or ice—is to put your developing solution into a metal or other container and place it in the refrigerator. Check it regularly and remove it when the temperature is right. Be sure to stir the solution well before arriving at your final reading, because the temperature will not be consistent throughout the liquid. If the temperature has gone below what was needed, it can be increased quickly by running warm or hot water on the outside of the container or using a warm water bath. This can be accomplished by filling a basin or other container with warm or hot water and swirling the container in it until its contents reach the required temperature.

To preserve the stability of stock solutions, store them at room temperature away from light. Camera stores sell brown plastic bottles and jugs that can be used for storage. However, it can be economical to reuse food containers such as bottles and jugs that have been thoroughly washed. Store these containers in brown paper bags in a closet. To reduce the possibility of oxidation, use containers of such size that after they are filled little or no space is available for air to come in contact with the liquid contents.

Always label your containers. Note the name of the chemical, its strength, developing times and temperatures, how much has been used, how much is left, the date it was originally mixed, and the dates portions were used.

If you have the opportunity to experiment under various picture-taking conditions, using different developers, you should do so. In that way you can zero in on what film, exposures, and chemicals are right for you.

Developers can be reused. But if they are, developing time must be increased for additional rolls of film. However, replenishers may be used to bring the solution back to its required potency.

Some developers are intended specifically for use with either film or paper; others may be used for both.

Overuse of the same solutions brings with it the risk that particles, as from sludge due to previous developing, may become embedded in your film.

After developing your film, the use of stop bath—an intermediate chemical—is recommended to wash the developer from the film and to slow down development. This prevents your hypo from becoming contaminated by large quantities of developer.

An improvised stop bath may be made by adding a couple of tablespoons of vinegar to a quart of water; the strength of the solution is not critical. Tap water can also be used for this intermediate step.

Hypo, or fixer, is the third solution. The time for use of these chemicals varies according to the specific product as recommended by the manufacturer.

After the use of hypo, the negatives may be exposed to the light. They are ready for washing.

The time required for washing can be reduced by the prior use of a clearing agent, which quickly removes excess hypo.

Following the wash, done according to the film manufacturer's package insert instructions, it is a good idea to rinse the film in a solution of a surface active agent, available at camera stores. This will prevent the occurrence of water spots.

Drying Negatives

Special clips are available for hanging film, but you can use a paper clip, pin, or other device, so long as you hang it free where it cannot come in contact with any surface. This can be done in a doorway, from the metal tubing that holds a shower curtain, or in any of a number of other places. Be certain that the air in the area in which the film is drying is free of dust particles.

To hasten the drying process, some photographers wipe excess drops of water from the film strip with a wet sponge or wet paper towel. However, this may cause scratching.

Drying Negatives Quickly

Drying time for hung film can be a half hour or more, depending on the surrounding atmosphere's heat and humidity. The process can be speeded up with the use of a hair dryer. But if you use one, set it at low heat and keep the nozzle at least six inches from the film, moving it along the strip on both sides. One end of the film should be fastened and the other held, or both ends fastened. High heat will reticulate the emulsion. Be sure to avoid dust.

How to Make an Inexpensive Film Dryer Easily

Speed is important to the press photographer—from picture taking at a spot news event to putting finished prints on the editor's desk. Film drying can cause a slowdown in the process. There are expensive dryers on the market that are used by professional photo labs, but their cost isn't usually justified for the freelance photojournalist.

For my own use, I devised a dryer that I made inexpensively and easily with materials that can be obtained at almost any hardware store or lumber yard. Cost for this dryer is in the vicinity of $1.

To make this film dryer, all you need is a small strip of aluminum sheeting, which is strong and malleable; a roll of duct (or heat) tape; two giant-sized paper clips; a pair of small shears; an ice pick; a ruler; a hammer; and a pencil.

If you have had experience with heavier metal sheeting and the tools required for working with it, you can construct a

1. Components used in making one-reel dryer. Top: roll of duct (or heat) tape. Strip below: metal to be made into cap. Strip below that: metal to be made into dryer body. Left, bottom: metal strips to support shelf disc. Left, middle: shelf disc, cardboard. Right, bottom: giant paper clips. (Not shown: disc with hole, to insert nozzle.)

sturdier dryer out of galvanized tin or even stronger sheet metal. Nevertheless, any metal will provide you with an effective dryer.

Because 35mm is the most commonly used film, the directions provided here are for a reel of this size. However, for other size films an adjustment of the height of the dryer is the only change that is necessary, since most reels are the same diameter.

The heating and blowing device used to operate this dryer is your hand-held hair dryer; or, better still, your canister vacuum cleaner. But, when using the vacuum, you must attach the hose to the exhaust in the rear for filtered air; otherwise, dust will be drawn over the film.

After constructing the dryer, you may want to check it for minimum drying time. The time will vary, depending on different factors—primarily the heat produced by your external system. You may find that your film has dried after four minutes, or possibly in as little as three minutes or less. A dryer body that holds more than one reel will take slightly longer. If you have a spare strip of old film handy, you can experiment with that until you have determined the exact drying time.

The diagram shown here provides instructions for constructing three different dryer bodies—for one, two, and three reels. Only one cap need be made; it will fit all three.

2. Top, left to right: dryer bodies for one-reel, two-reel, and three-reel. Bottom: cap, which fits each.

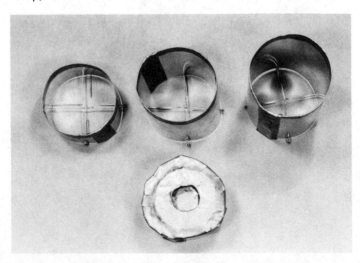

FILM DRYER

SCALE = 50%

BODY

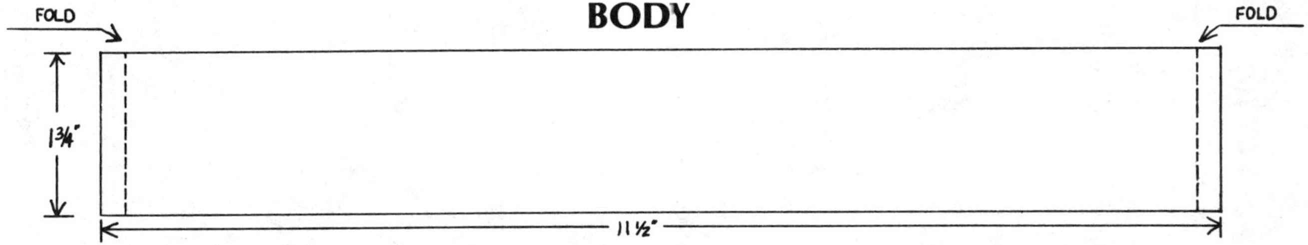

FOLD

FOLD

11½"

1¾"

CAP

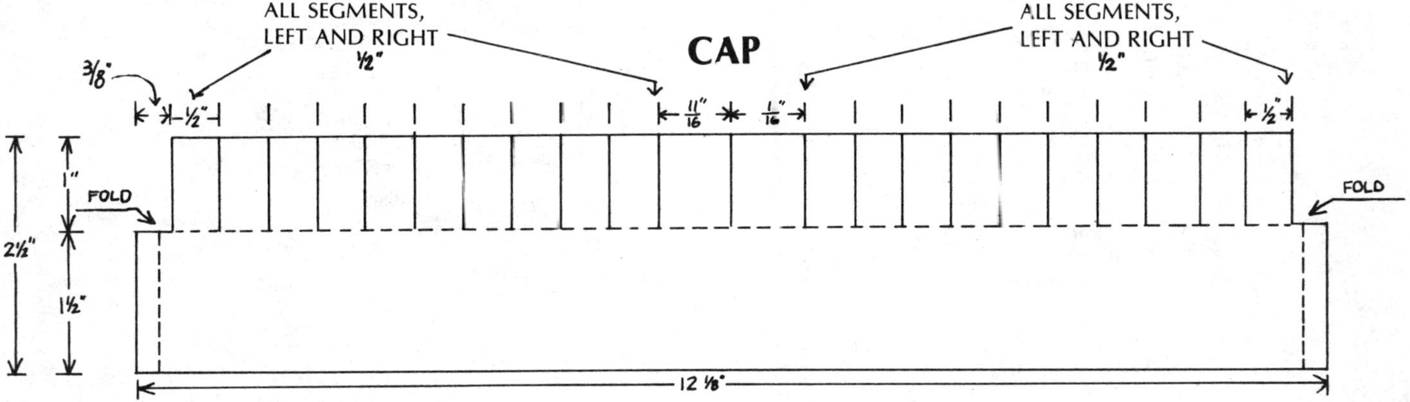

FOLD

FOLD

ALL SEGMENTS, LEFT AND RIGHT
½"

ALL SEGMENTS, LEFT AND RIGHT
½"

1/16"

11/16"

1/16"

3/8"

½"

1"

1½"

2½"

12 ⅛"

STRIP

FOLD

½"

½"

¾"

SIDE VIEW—FOLDED

The Dryer Body

The strip of metal used for the body should be 11½ inches long. Added to its width of 1½ inches for each reel, there should be ¼ inch to allow insertion of the bent paper clips, which will support one or more reels. Consequently, a one-reel dryer should measure ¼ inch plus 1½ inches, or 1¾ inches in height; a two-reel dryer, 3¼ inches; a three-reel, 4¾ inches; and so on.

Fold ¼-inch strips on each end of the metal strip, with flaps facing in opposite directions, as illustrated. This can be done simply by placing the metal over the edge of a ruler and bending it with your fingers.

Following the curvature of the metal, form a cylinder. This will provide the exact diameter needed for the 35mm developing reel—3⅜ inches. Place the two flaps together and press tightly until they hold fairly well. You can make the seam more secure by hammering it from the outside while bracing the inside against a solid object such as the shaft of a thick screwdriver.

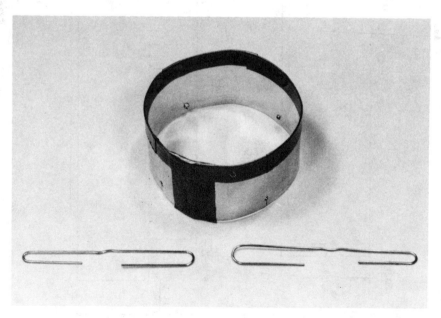

3. Dryer body with holes punched and giant paper clips bent and ready to insert.

Cut a strip of duct tape approximately ¾ inch wide and cover both sides of the seam.

Punch four evenly spaced holes, each pair diametrically opposed, ¼ inch above the rim. Make the holes just large enough for the paper clips.

Run a strip of tape around the other rim (short strips are easiest to work with), overlapping it and covering the edge of the interior and exterior by about ¼ inch.

Open the ends of two paper clips and slip them through the holes so that they intersect at right angles, then close them, as illustrated. This provides a supportive base for the film reel and an open passage through which warm air can flow. It also allows water drainage.

4. Dryer body with giant paper clips inserted (upside down; reel is put in from other side).

The Dryer Cap

Cut a metal strip 12⅛ inches long and 2½ inches wide. Measure 1 inch of the width and mark with a pencil line across the entire length of the strip. From this line, measure ½-inch intervals from the line to the closest edge of the strip and mark with a pencil line. Then, with a pair of shears, cut each of these lines to the original line you drew 1 inch from the edge. Cut and remove the ½-inch segment from each end of the strip, as illustrated in the diagram.

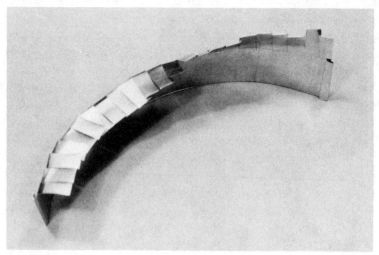

5. Dryer cap cut and partly bent into cylinder.

After cutting, fold each ½-inch flap to a 90-degree angle. Each flap will slightly overlap the one preceding it. As you did with the body, curve the metal strip, place the edges together, hammer, and secure with duct tape. Also, tape the interior between the flaps and sides of the metal cylinder so that when the cap is placed on the body, both taped areas will fit snugly.

From a piece of soft cardboard (the kind that backs note pads) cut out a disc smaller than the diameter of the cap, about three inches or slightly less.

Cut out a concentric circle within the disc, slightly larger than the size of the nozzle of the drying device you will be using, and put it aside. Place tape around the edges of the hole so that the opening is just tight enough for the nozzle to be inserted. Tape the disc with the hole onto the top of the cap. Now, take the smaller disc you cut out; it will be used as a shelf below the opening of the cap to enable the warm air to be evenly convected down the coiled film. To suspend this shelf beneath the hole in the cap, use four strips of the metal

6. Shelf disc with metal strips.

sheeting, each ¼ inch wide and 1¾ inches long. Bend them, as illustrated. Tape the ½-inch end of each with pairs diametrically opposed, as are the holes at the base of the body. The ½-inch portions of strips, which are bent perpendicular to the roof of the cap, suspend the disc.

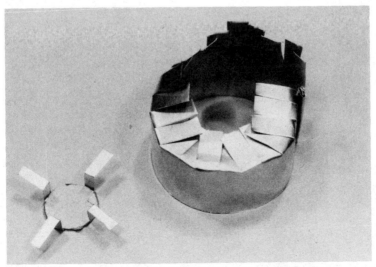

7. Shelf disc with metal strips and cap bent into cylinder.

Make certain that none of the cardboard is left exposed. It must all be covered by tape in order to avoid the possibility of loose fibers being blown into the wet film and becoming embedded.

When using this dryer, be certain not to use excessive heat. It might reticulate the emulsion, warp the film, or cause the gum on the duct tape to soften and stick to portions of the reel coming in contact with it.

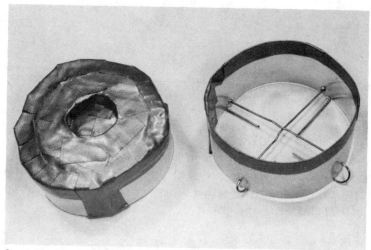

8. Completed dryer cap and dryer body.

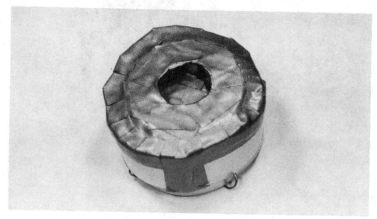

9. Dryer cap and dryer body put together.

10

Picture-Making: Proofs, Darkrooms, and Enlargements

How to Make a Proof

Being able to show a contact sheet to an editor gives the press photographer an edge. With a loupe—which is a special magnifier usually obtainable at any camera store—the positive 35mm frames can be examined closely, increasing the possibility of a sale.

Two types of photographic paper can be used for making proofs. One is contact paper, for which only a regular bulb is needed for exposure, and which can be used essentially without a basic darkroom. The other is enlarging paper, requiring the projected light of an enlarger, usually in a darkroom of some kind.

To make a print on contact paper, all that is needed are the following items: three 8-x-10-inch developing trays or their equivalent; a piece of glass, preferably a thick, heavy one; a darkroom safelight; and an electric lightbulb, about 60 watts. Tongs are also useful for transferring the paper from chemical to chemical.

Chemicals required are paper developer, stop bath (or a weak vinegar solution, or plain tap water), and hypo or fixer. An 8-x-10-inch piece of photo paper will accommodate up to thirty-six frames of 35mm film cut into strips of six frames each.

Place the negatives, emulsion side (dull side) down on the paper, with the paper's emulsion side (shiny side) facing up. Put the glass on top. Expose the paper with the lightbulb for several seconds. Initially, you will have to make a test for the required exposure by using a small piece of contact paper and at least one negative frame to determine the distance of the bulb and time required. After that, you should seldom, if ever, have to make another such test. However, negatives of slightly more or less density than normal may require different exposures. If the exposures on your film strip vary widely, it is best to make at least two proofs accommodating both extremes.

After exposing your negative strips, put the contact paper into the developer, emulsion side up, sliding an edge under the liquid first, then slipping the rest of the paper quickly after it so that it is totally immersed. You can lessen the risk of fogging by turning it face down. Agitate the solution during the recommended time for development. Transfer the paper to the stop bath or intermediate tap water wash. Rinse it vigorously for five or ten seconds to take off the excess developer and prevent excessive weakening of the hypo. Then transfer it to the hypo.

After the recommended fixing time, wash the proof in water for the length of time suggested by the paper manufacturer, let it dry—and you have your proof.

There are, of course, ways to make this procedure easier. You can buy a proofer, a device designed specifically for the purpose of making contacts. Many types are available. Basically, they are designed so that negative strips can be temporarily and conveniently fastened down in order to keep them parallel and uncurled. The glass either lies heavily on the negatives or can be snapped closed so that it presses tightly for sharp prints.

You can also buy or make a light box for producing contacts. This is a simple device with five sides, a top of glass, and a bulb inside. You put the negatives on the glass, emulsion side up, and the contact paper on that, emulsion side down. The paper is then exposed and developed the same as with the method using the piece of glass.

For making contacts with enlarging paper, an enlarger must be used. Using either a piece of glass or a proofer, as described earlier, the procedure is the same. Determining paper exposure requires initial experimentation regarding lens opening, the height of the enlarger, and the time of exposure.

Up to this point, you can still improvise without a darkroom.

Setting Up an Inexpensive Bare-Necessity Put-Up–Take-Down Darkroom

If you wish to progress to the step of actually making prints, you will need a darkroom. You can improvise one that you can set up and take down without too much inconvenience. And you can outfit it with minimal equipment at a low cost.

Naturally, the most important piece of apparatus will be the enlarger. A good one can be bought at a reasonable price in most camera or department stores or obtained used at considerable savings. If you have a room that is windowless, your primary problem in keeping it dark might only be light seepage around the door. Felt weatherstripping will block out any extraneous illumination.

If you use a windowless room, it would be most convenient to have one in which running water is available. Otherwise, it will be necessary to carry both water and chemicals, as well as trays, back and forth to your water supply for measuring and washing. Should this be your situation, it would be wise to place newspapers on the pathway between your darkroom and the water source. If this precaution is not taken, you may end up with chemical stains on your floor or rug.

If you have space available to set up your darkroom in a basement near laundry facilities, you will have the advantage of easy access to water and electricity. But you will need some kind of worktable. Additionally, you will probably be able to leave your apparatus set up for use for long periods of time because it will be out of the way.

A bathroom can be set up as a darkroom and dismantled in short order. Here is how to do this simply and efficiently.

A ¾-inch plywood sheet is cut to the width of the bathtub and about three-quarters of the tub's length. When placed across the tub it will allow a generous opening near the faucets for you to wash your prints in a tray above the drainpipe. A flat sink drain rack will prevent slippage of a tray for washing your prints in the tub and permit the water to escape easily.

The tub board will be for your three paper processing trays—developer, stop bath, and hypo. You will also have room on it for your enlarger if you don't mind stooping. Or you can put a low stool there for sitting.

This will leave the sink free for other water needs. However, if you have counter room on either side of it, the enlarger could be placed there at a convenient height. If this isn't possible, you can put a ¾-inch plywood piece on the sink itself for the enlarger and just use the tub as the water supply and wash area. An electrical outlet is usually conveniently available above the sink for shaving, minimizing the length of wire connected to the enlarger.

Should space be at a premium, try the toilet, lid down, for the plywood base and enlarger.

Thinner plywood (¼-inch) may be used to cover the window. Have a piece cut somewhat larger than the window frame so that it overlaps on all sides, touching the sill at the bottom. To ensure lightproofing, apply a strip of sticky-backed foam insulation—a width of about ½ inch is sufficient—around the edge of the surface that faces the wall. Clamps or bolts can be installed in such a way that the board may be easily removed after use.

When your darkroom has been completed, check its light-tightness by turning the lights off inside for about thirty seconds or so until your eyes adjust to the dark. If any isolated leaks are evident, they can be covered with opaque pieces of cardboard applied to the board and wall with easily removable masking tape.

Large darkroom bulbs are available that can safely light the entire room. A darkroom safelight can be suspended temporarily from the shower curtain tubing or elsewhere by any of a number of inventive methods. If your bathroom tile reflects your safelight excessively, you will have to cut down on the light by using a smaller bulb or by covering some of the light it produces. Paper exposed to a bright safelight for too long a period of time may begin to become fogged.

After use of the darkroom and its dismantling, the plywood sheets can be leaned against a wall out of the way or perhaps in a closet, where the enlarger can also be stored.

Darkroom equipment and supplies can be put into either a small cabinet in the darkroom or a closet or other storage area elsewhere.

In a matter of minutes, your darkroom has been restored to a bathroom—or whatever it was previously.

After the experience of having your own basic, improvised darkroom, you will be able to consider whether you will eventually want to put together a permanent, more thoroughly equipped one.

Making Enlargements for a Newspaper

Do newspapers have any special requirements for prints other than that they be about 5 x 7 to 8 x 10 inches? Yes, most definitely.

Basically, of course, the negatives of the photos should have been, to begin with, well exposed and in focus. But the technical work done on prints used for engraving is extremely important. That is one of the reasons most metropolitan newspapers employ darkroom personnel who deal principally with the developing and printing of pictures for staff and freelance photographers. Photofinishing is a specialized field. Of course, many press photographers, both freelance and employed, do their own darkroom work even when this convenient service is available to them at no cost. This is because some photographers prefer to use certain developers that are not readily available for use in the darkroom, where deadlines constantly loom and consistency is preferred. There, processing is usually done with established chemicals, papers, times, and temperatures. Besides, an excellent means of improving yourself as a photographer is constantly to adjust darkroom techniques and examine the results of each picture-taking experience to evaluate them.

Most importantly, a newspaper print must be dark. This does not mean that the entire photo should be overexposed by the enlarger, but that there should be as much contrast as possible. The range of grays should run the gamut between the extremes of pure white and jet black. A dark print for a newspaper is one in which each area has been brought out to its fullest printable limit of darkness. For example, a white shirt should not look bleached out; it should show folds and light and dark areas. A window in the background of a picture that, on the negative, shows objects beyond the glass should be printed so that those objects appear in the picture rather than being totally lost to whiteness. A close-up of a face should show delicate shadings if they exist on the negative.

A good way to see in detail exactly what is available on the negative is through close examination with a loupe. This magnifier is also useful for spotting dust, fibers, and other particles, which can then be removed with the use of film-cleaning chemicals, brushes, or by other means.

Often, just exposing the negative in the enlarger to the paper is not enough, because certain areas of the negative are denser than others, and exposing for one region can mean a loss in another.

However, darkroom techniques called *dodging out* and *burning in* can be used to overcome this problem. Usually, in fact, it is necessary to make more than one print in order to obtain the best results.

First, make a test strip. This is done by placing a small strip of enlarging paper across an area that has a wide range of shades. Then, using your hand or an opaque object, such as a piece of cardboard, block off segments at intervals of a few seconds. After processing the paper in the chemicals, select the best exposure. Test strip devices with windows of gradations that make the job easier are available.

For newspaper prints, dodging out and burning in are extremely important darkroom techniques that are employed regularly. Because there is a tendency for most newspaper engravings to make almost-dark areas darker and almost-light areas lighter, it is important that these intermediate areas be printed at exactly their optimum densities. Whenever one of your photos appears in print, in fact, you should always compare it to your original print with much scrutiny for future reference.

After making your test strips and determining exposure, make an initial print. After it has been in the hypo for the required length of time, study it under a bright light.

You may find it just right for submission. Or you may want to darken or lighten it in its entirety. Or, you may want to lighten or darken certain areas.

Sometimes a broad area of a picture should be darker. For example, a background in which tree branches, although they exist on the negative, are barely perceptible because of a whiting out. In such a case, you will probably want to reprint it better. To redo the photo for improvement, place your hand or a piece of cardboard or other object under the enlarger to block the light from the other sections of the picture after properly exposing the entire sheet of paper, allowing additional light to expose the paper where you want it darker. This is usually done about midway between the enlarger lens and the paper or near that point. To avoid a sharp demarcation, blending of densities can be accomplished by continual movement of the object.

Darkroom Techniques: Burning In and Dodging Out

Not all of your negatives are going to be ideal for printing; that is, some will require more photofinishing effort than just overall equal projection onto the enlarging paper. In some cases, an area of a negative will be exceptionally denser or thinner than the rest of the frame. This will require darkroom craftsmanship.

In these examples, a pilot I photographed (who literally holds a license signed by Orville Wright) had limited time to offer when I got together with him to take spontane-

Darkroom Techniques: Burning In and Dodging Out

ous outdoor portraits. Since I was unable, therefore, to start setting up and calculating for flash fill-in, I had to shoot quickly, getting what pictures I could in those few moments.

In the first photograph, the subject's cap cast a heavy shadow on his face. However, after processing the film, I was able to lighten his face and reveal detail by dodging out the shadowed area.

In the second photograph, I positioned him with a plane in the background, putting it slightly out of focus for effect. However, since he was in shadow and the plane was not, it was necessary to correct this print in the darkroom by burning in the aircraft.

You may not always get the results you want the first time. What you are doing by this process is burning in one area and dodging out another.

If complex areas of darkness and lightness need such work, you can burn in by using a piece of dark paper with a hole in it, which can be cut in any shape. Dodging out can be accomplished with a stiff wire or thin stick having a piece of cardboard at its top cut into a convenient shape and size. Inexpensive kits containing these components are available.

Sometimes a negative is overly dense or too thin to print on normal, or grade 2, paper. In such a case, other grades can be used. Special paper is also available that can be used under the same circumstances with contrast filters.

Always, then, if time allows, make the effort to dodge out and burn in to produce the best print you can. Your end product is what you are judged by, what encourages an editor to continue buying your submissions and give you assignments.

11

How *Not* to Take Press Pictures—Trial and Error

A photojournalist always learns by examining the results of previous misjudgments or by improving on techniques that were incorrectly used.

Sometimes after you trip your shutter, intuition—or, more likely, your intense observation at that instant—tells you that something went wrong. It might be the angle at which you photographed your subject, the lighting you chose, the exposure you calculated, an object you allowed to remain in the scene, or any other of a number of factors. If this is the case, you may be able to correct the situation immediately by taking the picture again, provided that the magical moment hasn't disappeared forever. You might even have the opportunity to retake the shot more than once.

Sometimes, however, you won't be that fortunate. You will discover only *after* you look at the developed negative that something went wrong. An excellent shot, one which can never be recaptured, will be lost because of a major flaw for which you were directly or indirectly responsible. In such a case, you will just have to remember not to allow such circumstances to occur the next time.

There are always new mistakes to be made in press photography. For this reason, photojournalism requires constant learning and self-improvement.

To illustrate this, here are some of the pictures I have taken which were flawed. Fortunately, I was able to correct some on the spot by reshooting them. Others taught me lessons for the future.

While photographing a literary event, I stole quietly down the aisle to get a picture of Harriet Adams, author of numerous Nancy Drew and Hardy Boys books. But before I could set my exposure and speed and focus the lens, she spotted me. Seeing that I wanted to take her picture, she most graciously turned to me and smiled. Because I wanted a candid shot of her unobserved, I snapped the picture she expected me to take, then waited. When she turned back to listen to the speaker, I got the picture I wanted.

Technical note: The film for these pictures was push-processed at ASA 1000 because they were taken under available-light conditions. (See Chapter 7.)

When taking pictures of fires, smoke always adds to your picture's dramatic quality, unless it obscures the scene. If a wind is blowing, shoot with it at your back, if possible. However, should the side where the smoke is heavy have more photographic possibilities, wait until the wind shifts before snapping from there.

At the fire depicted here, after I took my first shot from this particular viewpoint and saw the haze begin to be drawn away by air currents, I stayed at the same spot until I could see the damage that had been

caused by the blaze. Then I took another picture.

Burning in of the white area in the hazy picture will not show what was behind the cloud—on the negative there is just no image on the other side of the smoke! It appears dark on the emulsion.

After I had taken these and other pictures of the fire, I called a newspaper in a nearby large city and was asked to bring the film to them to develop. It was a sale.

I wanted to get a picture of this pastor outside his church for a newspaper article. In order to photograph both him and the church, including the steeple and cross—all in focus—I put my 24mm lens on the camera because a wide-angle lens not only condenses the view but offers a considerable depth of field. (With a normal 50mm lens, the background would have been out of focus at most exposures if I had stood close to him.) Looking through the viewfinder of my 35mm single lens reflex camera, after I had snapped the first picture, I realized that what I had

taken was more a snapshot than a professional picture for a newspaper. So I moved in closer and stooped farther below him, featuring him more and distorting the background with the angle. This compacted additional architecture, which is seemingly awry behind the subject, produces a more eye-catching effect for the newspaper reader.

This was one of four pictures selected by the department editor from those I submitted for the Sunday feature story.

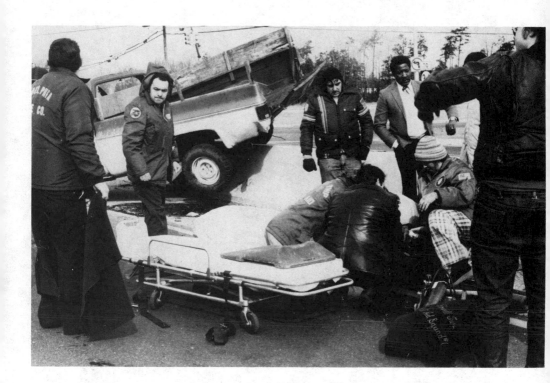

It is not always easy to photograph a victim during a first aid incident. But if you bide your time, are prepared, and position yourself where you might possibly accomplish your goal, with luck it can happen.

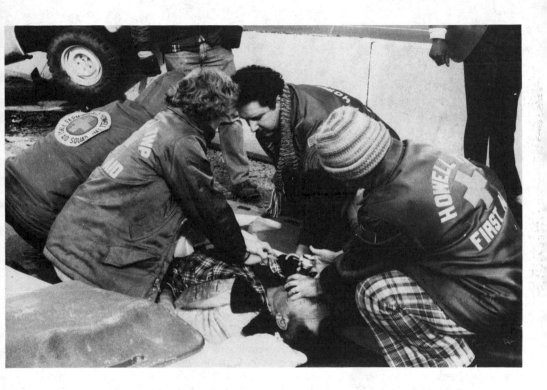

A picture showing the backs of emergency workers, even in a dramatic setting, does not have the impact of human identification.

Reproduced here are two pictures I took out of about twenty on an assignment at a high school basketball game. One shows a moment of peak activity: a player is about to toss the ball while two opponents are attempting to block him. This picture is not a good one for a newspaper because the players in the foreground are virtually inactive. The shot captures an interesting climax, but it unfortunately cannot be saved with cropping because, no matter how it is framed to make the major subjects large, disembodied legs will appear in the foreground.

The second shot shown here, one of a number of usable others taken at the same game, shows action in the foreground.

If you have a tight sports deadline to make in the evening for the next day's paper, it is often necessary to leave after the first fifteen minutes or so of a game. And since the ratio of usable shots to those taken is usually low, you should get as many good shots as you can. When you take pictures of sports activities, you often can't be sure of what you have until

the film is developed.

For indoor sports, I try to keep my ASA rating to a maximum of 1000. However, some gymnasiums are so poorly lighted for picture taking that I have to go higher. These photos were taken at ASA 1600. As a result—at least using the particular developer that I did—the white sections of the players' socks were lost against the brightness of the floor. Still, the results were better than they would have been with flash, which gives flat lighting, heavy shadows, and black backgrounds. Experimentation with film and developers can overcome problems and improve your results.

Whether in sports, or any other area, never become complacent about technique or materials. Always be willing to try something new. I subsequently changed to a developer that didn't bleach out basketball players' socks at a high ASA.

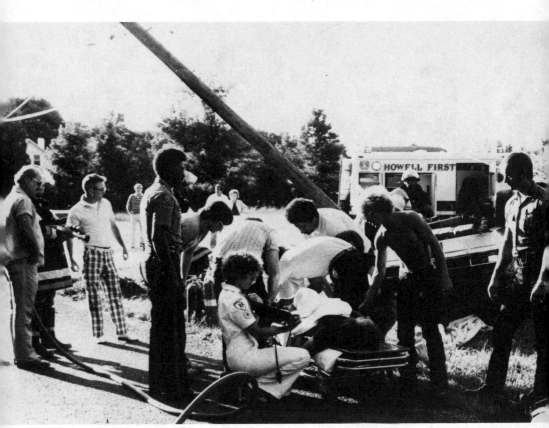

The victim of this accident involving an overturned car had to be extricated by a first aid team. Although I took shots from various points, the best position was from the viewpoint shown in the photo. Visible are the victim, emergency workers, police, ambulance, and overturned car. However, this photograph had to be taken almost fully against the sun.

When taking my meter reading, I didn't compensate enough for the backlighting. As a result, the figures are underexposed. Another *f*-stop wider was probably all that was needed to obtain textured grays rather than blacks in the foreground. Flash fill-in could also have been used to lighten up the foreground.

This picture was printed on the front page of a local tabloid. Despite its deficiencies in exposure, it had more to offer than other shots of the same accident that were properly exposed.

12

The Working and Business Sides of Newspaper Photography

The freelance photojournalist covering spot news or features on spec or assignment must be professional in dealing with the public on one hand and the newspaper on the other.

Caption information and other facts surrounding photographs taken must be exact. Locations must be precisely given and names correctly spelled.

The self-employed press photographer must be ethical and open with editors. A common understanding should exist at the start of business dealings regarding whether pictures of a single incident may be offered elsewhere at the time they are submitted, or later, and what payment is to be. In situations where agreed-on conditions are varied there should be complete awareness about what these changes are with both the photographer and editor.

As a freelance photographer covering news and features, you will often find yourself working closely with the general public, officials, statesmen, and celebrities and other notables, as well as with reporters and newspaper staffers. Each of these people will put his or her trust in you and your work. Your honesty and accuracy will carry a great deal of weight.

The Stringer

The term *stringer* was originally used to describe a part-time newspaper reporter whose copy, sent from a remote point, was measured for payment by the column length with a string. Today, it is also used as a designation for a nonstaff photographer who regularly supplies newspapers and wire services with pictures both on speculation and on assignment.

The stringer works for competing news markets and therefore must be highly ethical in dealing with editors.

The freelance press photographer, after obtaining spot-news photos to be submitted on spec, must evaluate certain factors in order to decide on a market or markets. These include the following: How important is the event? Is it primarily of local interest? Is it news or feature material on a broad scale? Regional? National? International? Which market will most likely pay the most? Which market would be more prestigious (a step forward for credits, career)? Which editors have been giving assignments or will more likely do so if given news pictures that they might not ordinarily obtain? What is the cost and time required to go to each of these editors? How do expenses balance out with expected payment? Which editors might be interested in the specific subject? Are the pictures exceptional in subject, allowing a bargaining edge? Should they be offered to more than one market? These and other aspects of your dealings with editors—some perhaps personal—must be considered.

There are also other points for the press photographer to consider from the viewpoint of the editors. Might any of them have sent a staff photographer or stringer to the event? Is there a staff photographer regularly covering—or living in—that area? Are there other freelancers near that location? Might a wire service photographer supply market needs? After weighing these considerations, the freelance press photographer begins making phone calls.

When on assignment, the freelancer must keep confidential the subject he is covering for that particular newspaper, get the work done swiftly and carefully, and report in as soon as possible with the raw film or prints.

Getting Caption Information

Always carry a note pad or blank paper in a pocket or in your camera bag, along with a pencil or pen. Always record immediately the names of subjects and informative facts about the pictures you are taking. Sometimes it is impossible to obtain these basic data later.

One way of keeping track of people you are photographing is to mark down corresponding film and frame counter numbers as noted in Chapter 15. If there is more than one person, note their positions from left to right. If there are any distinguishing physical characteristics, types of clothing, or actions of any individual in a particular shot, a word will pinpoint it for identification after the negatives have been developed.

You should obtain as much information for the editor as possible: the subjects' full names, what towns they are from, and their titles, if any. If you have photographed children, it is always a good idea to note their ages. Any other information that will serve to satisfy a reader's curiosity should also be recorded.

Contacting the Editor/Keeping in Touch

For spot news, immediately after taking your pictures call the newspaper and tell them what you have. If it is too early in the day, and you can process the film in your own darkroom, you might as well go ahead with it. In that way you can describe your picture to the editor in more detail from the negative than from what you remember.

Sometimes, if the news or photo editor is unavailable, you can leave information with an assistant or other staff member to be relayed. A phone call about your spot news photos benefits both you and the editor. The editor may have sent a photographer to the event, might be expecting photos from another photographer, or just might not be interested.

On the other hand, you may be tipping off the editor about an important event. As a result, while you are on your way to your darkroom or directly to the newspaper, reporters can begin digging up and putting together facts to surround your picture.

As for assignments, if you run into any problems or delays, always call the editor. There may have to be a change in deadline before you leave the assignment location to head back with whatever photos you have, or there may be a change in plans for the story—as drastic as postponing or killing it.

Whether you have taken a spot news photo or are on assignment, always let the editor know of your whereabouts and provide as much information as possible about the subject of your pictures and the circumstances surrounding them.

Sometimes a news situation might change and you will be going back to the editor with pictures that are completely different from those anticipated. As a result, the editor should be informed of the change by phone before you leave the assignment location in order that the latest information be obtained to update the story.

At any rate, when you are on an assignment—especially at a good distance from the newspaper—letting them know by phone what pictures you have taken and when you expect to be at their editorial offices allows the editor to plan page makeup more effectively.

Editing Your Film

Who edits your pictures? Naturally, if the editor asks you to bring prints, you are the one who does the selecting and cropping of your photos. But there are some instances when the editor prefers to make the choices from the negatives.

If you are going to deliver finished work to the editor, it is always best to make a selection of at least two or three pictures—each as different from one another as possible. On the back of each, attach caption information. This can be done with a small slip of paper, fastened with transparent tape, on which the facts are written or typed. It should have the date, your name, address, and phone number, what the news event is, and who and/or what is in the picture. Also, if available, provide names and phone numbers that may be useful for obtaining further information. Make yourself a copy, preferably with carbon paper, for your files.

If your photos are of an important event, the editor might publish more than one, which may mean additional payment. That is why different shots should be submitted. For example, from pictures of a fire you might select an overall view of a burning building, another with a couple of firemen playing a hose on one section of the blaze, and perhaps an additional one of people whose lives have been affected by the tragedy.

Although cropping can give a picture impact, always allow extra area in order to allow the editor the option to crop as needed. There should be enough picture area so that it can fit within any planned space between columns—tending toward a horizontal or vertical shape or with its subject full enough to be used in cutout fashion, if desired.

If you filled your frame economically when you took the picture, you might want to provide it in its entirety. A 35mm frame is almost exactly in the same proportion as a 5 x 7 inch enlargement; printed on 8-x-10-inch paper, an extrawide margin will occur along one of the longer edges.

The Editor Says: "Use Our Darkroom"

You know that your work is wanted on a regular basis when an editor suggests that you use the newspaper's darkroom. This can result from a number of circumstances.

If the newspaper's staff photographers and/or technicians who process freelancers' film are busy, doing your own can provide quick results for consideration of the editor without risk of missing a deadline.

If you bring consistently usable work to a particular newspaper, a feeling of trust in your pictures will evolve. The staff will know that, in a pinch, time can be saved when you use their equipment and supplies.

The first time is always an awkward moment—working in unfamiliar surroundings, sometimes with a developer that you have seldom, if ever, used before.

When you are shown into the darkroom, ask all the questions that enter your mind about the equipment and supplies. Find out where the light switches are, how to lock the darkroom door, where the timer and safelight are located, how to operate them, and other related details. Be certain that you have been fully supplied with apparatus: a developing tank, proper reel, and means of opening your film magazine. Be sure that you have been fully informed about the chemicals. Where are they located? Is the developer fresh or used, requiring additional developing time? Where is the running water? What about regulation of temperature? Dryer? How does the enlarger work? Where is the enlarging paper?

Most importantly, ask about the developer you will be using. Which is it? Should it be diluted with water? What time and temperature does the newspaper use with it?

Sometimes, if your photos are of an important news event, reporters might be putting the story together as you are doing your darkroom work. Therefore, the editor will find it helpful if you provide general caption information before you go into the darkroom. Then, after the negatives have been developed and you have made your selections, let the staff know in some detail about those specific choices. Sometimes it is also helpful for a newspaper staff to be informed about whether the best picture is vertical or horizontal.

The next time around, you will practically be an old hand at working there.

Working with a Reporter

There may be occasions when you will meet with a reporter on an assignment. This will be of great benefit to you because that person, as the writer of the article you are illustrating, is familiar with facts beyond what has been written and, while in your company, will probably be seeking out more information that can be of use to you.

Although you will no doubt be given excellent suggestions for photos by the reporter, don't use the opportunity to take a mental vacation. Think about various other possibilities, discuss them with the reporter, and make suggestions of your own.

Many times a writer will assume that the editor has told you what pictures the newspaper wants and will offer no suggestions. In such instances, it is a good idea to describe to the reporter the shots you have in mind and ask if any beyond that are desired.

Writing Sells Photography

Newspaper copy and photography are complementary elements of journalism. Quality performance in each area requires the acquisition of basic occupational knowledge and experience and the constant practice and development of related skills.

It is possible to cultivate abilities in both of these areas of journalism. And, in fact, when this is done, they enhance each other and provide advantages for the writer-photographer.

Some newspapers buy feature packages from freelancers. You should ask your local editors about this. Or you might want to put one or two combination photo-articles together first on spec for submission to them.

Subjects for these photo-illustrated feature stories are unlimited. They can cover such topics as a local personality who has an interesting background, local projects for the elderly or disadvantaged, location shooting of a movie, and many other stories that can give newspaper readers an insightful glimpse of their own residential area.

As both writer and photographer, you have the advantage of conceiving picture ideas on your own to illustrate the written points of your piece that you wish to emphasize.

When submitting such combination material, always supply

an editor with a good selection of pictures from which to make choices for a layout. To save yourself time and expense, a contact proofsheet is often a good way to submit your pictures. If an editor is not too familiar with the quality of your finished work, you might include a couple of sample prints.

In addition to bettering your chances for selling your photographs, the writing itself can also bring you income.

Picture stories, after they are published, are good possibilities for spin-offs to magazines. And an advantage to offering them is that you can send a photocopy of your piece, which shows that it has been published.

How Much Do Newspapers Pay for News Photos?

Payment for news and feature photos varies widely. It can range from nothing up to substantial hourly and flat rates, with expenses included or paid separately. Expenses can include mileage (on a per-mile basis or as a flat rate for stringing from a particular area), film (or replacement of it), tolls, phone calls, parking, and other related items.

The payment that you can expect depends on many factors. It is determined by the size and circulation of the newspaper, the budget for freelance purchases, and policies regarding how much spot news a particular newspaper will accept from freelancers. There are usually going rates. The number of full-time staff photographers will have a strong bearing on policy regarding photos accepted on spec and the number of assignments given to outside photographers.

Local tabloids often cannot afford to pay at all, or they have a very low flat rate of payment per picture. Many larger newspapers, as well as the wire services, also have a flat rate for a news photo, but it is, of course, much higher. Sometimes the amount paid is on a sliding scale ranging from a set amount for an average shot to a limit for an extraordinary picture.

Assignments, as opposed to news photos submitted on spec,

bring the freelance press photographer guaranteed payment. Assignment rates are usually similar to a newspaper's spec rates. In some instances, a newspaper will pay a series of set prices for acceptance of more than one picture. For example, there will be a base rate for the first picture, which will be the major payment; then, for additional photos used—taken on the same assignment—there will be bonus payments per picture.

Some newspapers pay an hourly rate plus expenses for assignment photos, with a basic minimum should your assignment run so smoothly that you wind it up quickly. Assignments, however, can take longer than expected because of delays, unavailability of persons involved, and other factors. Should this happen, you should always let the editor know. Copy and photo editors understand that problems can arise on a photo assignment and will usually compensate you for extra time and expense. But you can't expect them to do this unless they are informed about it; otherwise, they will assume, and rightly so, that all went well on the job they assigned to you.

Model Releases

Model releases are usually not required for people in news event photos used for newspapers, magazines, or books; they are needed, however, for pictures used in advertising. Sometimes, editors ask that you supply releases in certain sensitive situations, such as for classes involving handicapped children, or incarcerated subjects. A newspaper may, in fact, supply its own release forms.

Occasionally, at an assignment the photographer will be requested to take pictures so that the subjects' faces are not recognizable. This is usually done, of course, by taking the pictures from behind the subjects; however, it can also be accomplished with lighting or by physical blockage with props at the setting.

Standard model release forms that you may copy and use without obtaining permission are available in any number of books on photography, as well as through organizations for photographers.

If you have any questions about whether a release is needed in any situation, always check as far in advance as possible with the editor.

Copyright and Negative Ownership: Sale and Resale Rights

Who owns your negatives and the right to use them? Each newspaper and wire service has its own policies. In some circumstances, the photographer and editor may arrive at an overall agreement. Specific terms might be reached in particular instances. However, in general, the situation is as follows:

A freelancer who delivers spot news on spec to a newspaper owns the negatives and their copyright. He sells the rights for one-time use unless otherwise agreed.

In some instances, as perhaps with a wire service, the rights to the picture are owned jointly. Therefore, each owner may sell one-time rights at any time in the future.

The freelancer owns the negatives, unless otherwise agreed to with the editor. However, the editor may request ownership of the frame used.

Usually, the news organization that gives a photographer an assignment owns these negatives and the right to use and reuse them and offer them for sale. There are, of course, variations on these rules. Sometimes, though a newspaper owns the rights to negatives, if it uses another picture from an assignment (or spec submission), the newspaper will pay the photographer an additional sum. In other cases, a newspaper will allow a photographer on assignment to own the negatives and copyright.

If you own your negatives and the rights to use them, under U.S. copyright law it is generally recognized that you own the copyright without the need for formal registration. There are ways, however, that you can lose your copyright ownership to public domain, such as through display or reproduction without copyright notice. If you wish to learn more details about this or to have legal documentation regarding copyright ownership, contact the federal copyright office. Information about copyright will be sent free, including specific facts about filing, which requires application and fee. For pertinent facts and necessary forms, write to: Copyright Office, Library of Congress, Washington, DC 20669.

If you own the rights to the sale of your pictures, you may sell one-time rights many times over, as long as that is your agreement with each purchaser.

Always have a clear understanding with every editor with whom you deal as to who owns the negatives of the pictures you took and the rights to use them.

Billing the Editor

The standard procedure for dealing with newspapers on a business basis as a freelance press photographer requires monitoring of the newspapers and billing of the editors for work published or assigned.

Payment is not usually sent automatically after a photographer's work appears in print. You must bill the editor.

Occasionally, your accepted picture might not be published in a first edition. Be sure, therefore, if your submitted work does not appear in your copy, to check other editions. If this is not possible, call the newspaper's editorial department and check it out. A photo I once took appeared in print well over a year after I submitted it. I billed the newspaper and was paid.

In your bill, expenses that are related—according to your arrangement with that newspaper—should be listed.

Information provided in the bill should pinpoint the news event so that it can be recalled or located easily in a back issue. These facts should include as much of the following as possible: slug (the word under which the accompanying article was filed or stored in the computer), date of assignment, person assigning the job, date photos were taken, and— if useful to the editor—the time spent traveling and photographing. You should also specifically note the date and page number of the publication of your work—and the number of photos used, if your payment is related to that.

Billing for assignments can be done immediately after completion of the work, even though it may be for a feature piece scheduled for much later publication. However, you may want to wait until your work appears in order to note the date and page on your bill—especially when the policy of the newspaper is to pay extra when more than one photo is used.

Some editors prefer that you add up the costs and assignment rate; others prefer to do this themselves. After your first sale to an editor, you should ask how the billing is to be done. Also, find out what the rates are for later use of the same photos or others that you hand in that are not used at that time.

Some editors will not pay at all if your pictures are not used, and they will usually inform you of this when you call to offer news photos. You might want to ask at that time about rates, if nothing is mentioned, since they might assume you know of their policy.

As for that once-in-a-lifetime spectacular photo (or more than once-in-a-lifetime one, if you are extremely fortunate—and ready), its prices and conditions for sale are strictly up to you and what the market will bear. Should you ever find yourself in such a position, good luck in your bargaining.

13

The Editor's Criteria

Depending on the staff size and circulation of a newspaper, there may be photo editors in addition to copy editors.

An editor has an overview of an article—what facts it covers, what the most important aspect is, and what changes may be taking place in the text just prior to its publication. In addition, the editor is aware of how it will be arranged on a page and how it will be in juxtaposition with other related or unrelated material. Also, when the page is made up, the editor has to calculate the amount of copy and the space available for photographic illustration.

All these factors, plus personal taste, of course, integrated with the opinions and experience of coworkers and the photos available for that story, figure into the final decision. Therefore, a photographer should provide the editor with as wide a choice of photos as possible from which to select, unless the concept of the photo has already been predetermined and requested by the editor. Even then, you should make every effort to supply the editor with more and additionally different shots than those requested.

A Free Course in Newspaper Photography

You can begin immediate study in the field of press photography by carefully going over area newspapers and looking at the pictures with a questioning and critical eye, rather than with the casual glance you may have been giving them until now.

Study your neighborhood tabloid, newspapers of somewhat higher circulation, and the larger ones that cover statewide news and international events. Go to a library where you can see issues of newspapers that are recognized as top-notch in the field of journalism.

Each level of newspaper has certain needs, and the more you look them over, the more you will absorb by osmosis what editors desire for the segment of the population for which they provide news.

Generally, local tabloids will cover the giving of awards, plaques, and checks, groundbreakings, and local political events. An area newspaper will be interested in automobile accidents and fires occurring within its domain, though they might not necessarily be exceptional. A large metropolitan newspaper will usually be interested in events of substantial import about which its readers many miles away would want to be informed.

Wire services prefer pictures that depict state or regional happenings and those occurrences, ranging from humorous to tragic, that dramatize the foibles of man or a universal scale with which anyone anywhere can identify.

As you look at each picture in these newspapers, consider how you might have covered the event. Which film would you have used? What developer? Would you have looked for another aspect of the subject to photograph? Would you have taken the picture from the same angle or used light differently? Would you have taken it horizontally or vertically?

From near or far? Would you have used flash? Are you satisfied with the composition? What about the cropping? If you had taken that picture and had been satisfied with it, how would you take it the next time to improve on it?

Apply these questions to your own photos after they come out of the darkroom and after they are published.

The One That Got Away

One of the most common experiences that you will have as a press photographer is regretting the picture that you didn't take. There are many reasons that you may not have taken that ideal photo.

Many times while traveling to an event you will anticipate possible results, but when you arrive you discover that nothing appears as you thought it might.

At the scene, you may wait for certain elements to come together in your viewfinder—in vain.

You might have your exposure set for one scene and quickly switch to another setting, not making or being able to make an adjustment.

You may be photographing from a position that may not have been the best, as it turns out.

Deadline may force you to leave a scene just when what is coming up promises to be what you were seeking.

However, a statement used in journalism applies not only to verbal information but to photographs: *go with what you have*. Do your best. Don't brood about your losses, but go on. Nobody is perfect—not even you. Besides, sometime when you are just doing a routine photography job—properly—fate will compensate you for those past misfortunes with an extraordinary setting or subject, perfect lighting, and an ideal vantage point, handing it to you on a silver platter.

Which One Did the Editor Choose?

One morning at 5:00 A.M., while I was listening to one of

my local radio stations—a usual practice that provides picture leads—an interesting news item was announced. An abandoned car (later reported to have been stolen) was dangling from a railroad bridge, blocking the track that carried a busy commuter line. The newscaster also said that a crane was to be brought to that location at 7:00 to remove the car so that heavy train schedules would not be disrupted when they began for the day. The time of the year was autumn, which meant that the sun would not rise until about an hour or so later.

According to my calculations, based on the maps I keep in my office at home, a trip there would take about forty-five minutes. Therefore, I would have time to wait for sunrise to take the pictures without flash. (Still, I took flash equipment with me, as I always do.) So there was no need to rush there.

I stopped off on the way at a gas station near my destination to ask about which side of the bridge I should drive to in order to avoid going too far from the incident. No one at the station had heard about the abandoned car.

I drove to the nearest side of the bridge and saw nothing unusual. To get to the other side, I had to go out of the way to cross a bridge for cars, which was parallel to the train bridge. On the other side of the river, I again drove to the railroad bridge, but I saw no car dangling.

By then it was already past 6:30 A.M. I walked to the edge of the bridge. Far in the distance was another bridge. Perhaps, I thought, that was the one where the action was taking place. If that was the case, I could try to get there before 7:00 A.M. But by that time, I figured, either the car would be gone or I might just capture the tail end of the event—removal of the car by the crane.

As I was about to turn back to my car to check out the other location, I looked over the edge of the bridge. Below was the car. Two policemen were standing by it.

I immediately pulled my camera out of my bag for grab shots. *Grab shots* are pictures taken immediately, without extensive planning, just in case the subject might suddenly no longer be available.

As usual, my camera was loaded with a 20-exposure roll of film having a 400 ASA rating—the most useful for all conditions. I had the wide aperture on my 55mm lens set at $f/1.2$, and my shutter speed was at its usual ready-for-action 1/125 second. All I had to do was turn on the camera, adjust the f-opening, lean on the parapet, and start shooting in the early dawn light.

The car was blocking the rails going south, but a train was just going north, so I quickly shot the first picture with the train in the background. When I noticed that there were wires across the picture (see contact proof sheet of this series), I moved forward to exclude them. The appearance of the wires would not have been detrimental to the finished pictures, but I wanted a clear shot if I could get one. At frame 8, the last car passed my view. Then I took a final shot from the same point, even though there would be no train in the picture. It would show the surrounding water and the precarious position of the car (frame 9).

I then went to the embankment and shouted to the policemen, explaining that I was a press photographer and asking their permission to go down onto the tracks. I was told that I could, but that I should be extremely careful because of trains coming through.

Before descending to the tracks I noticed a sign that said "No trespassing" (frame 10, also shown as an enlarged print). Although there were some weeds in the foreground, the scene behind them couldn't have been posed better if I had arranged it. The car was clearly across the tracks, the policemen were discussing the situation, and behind them could be seen the drop-off into the water. I shot it immediately.

Once on the tracks, I replaced my 55mm lens with a 24mm wide-angle and took two shots along the tracks (frames 11 and 12) as the policemen went about their duties in readiness for the next train to pass by.

I then went to the car to see what other angles were possible. Standing at the rear of the car, looking through my viewfinder with the wide-angle lens attached, I saw a very

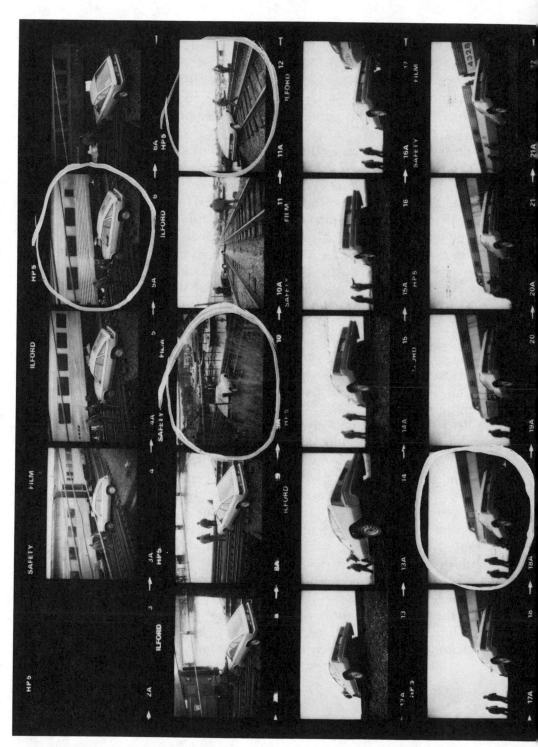

dramatic view waiting to be taken. The left rear tire was dangling from the track.

I focused the camera, still set at 1/125 second, and shot the picture just as the policemen disappeared behind the car (frame 13). I wanted them to add to the picture composition, so, as I waited there for them to reemerge, I moved to slightly different points in order to exaggerate the rear of the car so that I could create the best dramatic effect possible. While doing this, I also attempted to capture the subjects as they made interesting gestures (frames 14 through 16)

Then I saw that a train was about to come through. To avoid blurring, I set my shutter speed at 1/250 second. The lighting was very tricky. The sun was still not above the horizon. I was shooting dark subjects and a dark area against sky that was already lit.

To set my exposure, I aimed my camera at the ground, which was as dimly illuminated as my subjects and would, therefore, give me a similar meter reading. At 1/250 second, a correct exposure required an $f/2$ opening—the limit of my lens. (Had conditions necessitated a larger opening, I would have had to go with a slower speed—blurring or not. Of course, I could have exposed for push-processing, but that would have meant taking the time to change the film because the roll I was using was already exposed at ASA 400.)

I decided to finish out the roll with a series of shots as the policemen guided the train through (frames 17 through the end).

As soon as I returned home, I developed the film and printed a contact proof from which I made my choices.

Since this was an oddball happening, I thought I might offer it to more than one market. The first would be a large metropolitan newspaper I deal with regularly. I also had in mind a wire service with a bureau office in the same city. For that reason, I made four choices from my proof rather than my usual two or three.

I made 5 x 7 prints. I find this a convenient size with which to work; 8 x 10 is also a commonly used size. Although newspapers have the facilities to reduce and enlarge prints on the spot to a size required for page makeup, it is best to find out in advance which size a particular newspaper favors.

Some time after 10:00 A.M., which is about the time most large newspaper staffs begin to assemble, I called the newsroom, told them about the event, and described my pictures. They were interested.

I then asked if, after allowing them the first selection, they would mind if I then offered dissimilar choices elsewhere. I specifically noted my market plans. In this instance, I was told that they preferred exclusivity, so that was our arrangement. Had the news event been one of greater importance, I would have been in a different position in making my offer. In such instances, too, prices can also be negotiable, rising above the going rates.

But keep in mind that if you sell to a wire service, a

A

newspaper subscribing to that service will receive the photo-graph not long after it has been accepted. Some newspapers may prefer to buy an exclusive frame rather than use the same picture that the wire service bought; others may not, which is why you must be clearly informative in dealings with editors.

Newspapers subscribing to wire services are usually required to supply any photos requested by that service. However, there are times when a newspaper will release a staff photo of spot news for use over the wire, but only beyond a radius of perhaps fifty miles in order to ensure that it cannot be used by competitive publications.

I brought the four choices shown (which might have been different selections if they had been yours) to the newspaper. Which one do you think the photo editor bought?

Answer: A. I learned that it was chosen because of the train in the picture and its position.

B

C

D

Your Pictures Were Accepted But Not Used

You worked hard—either on spec or on assignment—spent time taking pictures, used your equipment, film, and perhaps darkroom materials. Result: the editor accepted your pictures. But when you looked in the newspaper the next day, your work wasn't there. Why?

There are a number of reasons a picture, though of good quality, may not be used, through no fault of your own. Often, on spot news, an amateur or assignment photographer for a wire service was there, and before the newspaper was put to bed the editors making up the page received their photo and favored it over yours.

In other instances, more important news and/or photos came in at the last moment and displaced your photography which had been planned for publication.

You can console yourself with the fact that this also happens to the work of staff photographers. They, however, have guaranteed salaries.

Do you get paid when photos are accepted and not used? Again, circumstances vary with each newspaper as well as the situation, which will in some instances depend on your relationship with the particular editors with whom you deal.

First, let's consider the spot news situation. You covered a news event on your own and called the editor. The editor told you to bring the undeveloped film, or prints, to the newsroom. In most cases, such an invitation guarantees you minimum payment whether or not the picture is published. It may even bring you the full amount paid for a published picture whether or not it is used. But it may also bring you no payment at all.

In some instances—and you may be forewarned on the phone—there will be payment only if the picture is used. Some editors may still pay you expenses if the picture is not used. Some may not.

An assignment is a different situation. Whether your photos are used or not, you will be paid.

WHICH ONE DID THE EDITOR CHOOSE?

I learned of a writers' conference, through the usual ads and brochures, that was to be given at the New Jersey Institute of Technology. But what made this particular occasion special was that faculty member Dr. Herman A. Estrin was establishing a state authors' Hall of Fame.

I contacted the book editor of an area newspaper for which I had done freelance work and suggested doing an article on spec, with pictures. There was interest and a go-ahead. Plans were made for the package to be preprinted for a Sunday edition so that it would appear the day after the occasion.

I arranged to get together with Dr. Estrin and, with my wife, Audrey— with whom I sometimes collaborate—we all met in Newark for our

interview. There, after a taping session, I took pictures of Dr. Estrin in his office and inside and outside the library where a scroll of the authors' names and a collection of their works would be housed.

After processing the pictures, I selected two and submitted them. From those, the editor chose one for a text-picture layout that filled half a page.

Which picture do you think was used?

Answer: The photo used was the one taken outside the library.

NOTE: Subsequently, this photo was submitted to a regional state magazine with two others for another article being done on Dr. Estrin. It was again bought for use (one-time rights).

WHICH ONE DID THE EDITOR CHOOSE?

C

When a photo editor makes selections from your negatives, not all of the choices are necessarily used. Just as you would turn in a few photos for the selection of one, if that is a requirement of a newspaper, so does the photo editor usually provide a selection for final choice at page makeup time.

Here are three of my pictures selected by a photo editor of a regional New Jersey newspaper. Which one do you think went to press?

Answer: photograph C.

On early morning local radio I had heard of a charred body found after an overnight house fire. When I arrived at the scene, the atmosphere was somber as firemen and investigators examined the site.

After taking the pictures, I called a large circulation state newspaper and was asked to bring my film to their photo lab for development.

The atmosphere of the selected picture, etched onto the film with a wide-angle lens (24mm), was no doubt what inspired the caption writer to title it "Grim Scene."

A

B

   Camper Destroyed. Early one morning, a while before dawn, I heard a call over my scanner (police, fire, and first aid radio) that a mobile home was on fire. I rushed to the scene. In the short fifteen minutes it took me to get there, the vehicle had been reduced to a sketeton—and the firemen started off to the fire scene when I did. I used a flash with a high voltage battery pack, which can recycle (charge up for a new picture) in a fast sequence. As a result I was able to shoot many pictures of the scene from various angles. This gave me a wide selection of shots from which to choose. (I also stepped back off a low garden wall from which I was taking pictures, and fell into a huge puddle of water. But I held my camera up high as I tumbled, and it was all right. Neither was I hurt. Two firemen came to my rescue.) Almost every shot on the entire roll of pictures would have been saleable. I selected the two best, from which the newspaper made a choice. Here they are. Can you guess which one was published?
   Answer: photo B.

A

B

Autumnal Scene. When a new season is upon us, sometimes a newspaper likes to depict its arrival in a photographically poetic way for its readers. I was coming back from a fire call announced on my scanner, which had been nipped in the bud by firemen, when I saw these two young boys coming down the road next to a wooded area. I pulled my car over and asked them if they would let me take some shots of them with the horse, in the woods, for possible publication in a local paper. They were pleased to pose. I submitted two photos; one was used. Which do you think it was?

Answer: photo A.

WHICH ONE DID THE EDITOR CHOOSE?

A

B

School Bus Mishap. This unusual incident happened only about a mile from where I live. A freak accident such as this always has appeal for a newspaper reader. In order to fit both vehicles into my picture as tightly as possible, I used my 24mm lens. There were only two angles that presented the best overall views—from the front of the bus and from the back. Since students were still on the bus, I asked them to open the windows and lean out—to give the picture a human element. Naturally, they gladly did this. Fortunately, no one had been hurt. Which of the two photos submitted do you think was sold?

Answer: the one taken from the back of the bus, photo B.

A

B

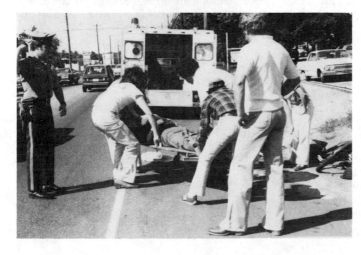

C

WHICH ONE DID THE EDITOR CHOOSE?

Bicyclist Injured. First aid squads usually follow a certain emergency strategy to have personnel on the scene as soon after an accident as possible. Members nearest an accident report directly to the scene to give the victim immediate attention and provide any first aid necessary before transportation to the hospital; others report directly to headquarters, from which the ambulance and/or extrication equipment is dispatched. In this particular accident involving a car and a bicycle, I arrived after two of the first aid people but before the ambulance. I shot a roll of film, covering the arrival of the ambulance through its departure with the victim, and turned three photos in to a local paper. Later, I offered the same three photos to a magazine that publishes accident photos for paramedic and first aid readers. Each selected a different photo from the same three submitted. Can you guess the choices of the newspaper and magazine?

The newspaper chose a photo showing the bike (A), which made it clear that a local bicyclist was involved. The magazine, mainly interested in first aid, showed the people alone under stress (B).

NOTE: My local township bought two prints, after seeing it in the newspaper, so that they could show evidence that the roadway needed improvement. And, in addition, I subsequently resold one (again, one-time rights) to accompany an article I wrote on first aid—to another newspaper.

It pays to make friends with emergency people.

One morning at dawn, I turned on my scanner and heard follow-up talk about a fire that had evidently occurred overnight and been brought under control. No further information was forthcoming, however, to help me identify the location. So I called a friend who is a member of the local first aid squad. After obtaining the address of the fire scene, I went there immediately with my camera.

Arson was suspected. A bible school had been gutted. On the scene were the pastor and an investigator from the local fire prevention bureau.

For taking pictures, one position provided an ideal camera viewpoint. It was at the doorway, looking at the destruction of the building's interior against the open sky (the roof was gone). The sun was just coming up, requiring a wide aperture—even with a fast film.

I asked the men if they would kindly pose for me against the scene. They both agreed. I put a 24mm wide-angle lens on my camera and took three series of pictures. In the foreground, I photographed each man separately, and both together.

I returned home, developed the film, made my selections, and made prints. I called the photo editor at a metropolitan newspaper nearby. There was interest. I dropped off these three photos. Which one do you think was published the next day?

Answer: the picture of the pastor.

14

How to Take Accident Photos/Fire and Auto

Fire Pictures

Ironically, the biggest blaze can give you a boring, unsaleable picture, if it isn't photographed properly. On the other hand, at a fire of less consequence your camera can produce eye-catching photographs, if you use your imagination, creativity, artistic skills, and ingenuity.

It is important to capture the drama of a fire in such a manner as to convey to the newspaper reader a feeling of actually witnessing what has occurred, even though it is a vicarious experience.

First of all, you as a photographer should get as close to the fire as possible without threat to your safety.

Police lines will usually be set up immediately on arrival of fire fighting equipment, and police or fire personnel will stand guard. The boundaries blockaded are established as far away from the fire as possible, which means that it is still not a risk for you to be somewhat closer. Therefore, as a photographer you may be able to move in closer.

If you have a press card from a local paper—and it can sometimes be obtained from just an area tabloid that carries local advertising—you may find it effective in allowing you to get near enough to the action, for a reasonable time, to take your pictures. If this doesn't work, explaining to officials holding back the crowd that you are a freelance press photographer might bring you several yards closer to where it's all happening, which can be a plus factor.

Fire photos taken from a long distance will show a lot of uninteresting open space around the actual blaze or total building, only part of which may be on fire. As a result, a wide perimeter of your photo will be of streets, houses, sky, and people and firemen just standing around doing nothing.

If you have a telephoto lens of 135mm or more, you will have better odds of obtaining good pictures on either side of the fire lines. A telephoto zoom of about 80 to 200mm is of additional advantage. These lenses also come in handy if you are permitted to go a reasonable distance toward the fire, because they will permit you to get close-up shots of firemen at upper-floor windows.

With a zoom lens you will be able to move in and out on a scene and compose it dramatically. It is always best to crop (frame) your shot while taking it, rather than afterward. By cutting out the uninteresting perimeter of the scene you are photographing as you look through your viewer with a zoom on your camera, you can benefit in more than one way. This will give you impact, as well as greater detail, because you are making use of all of the film frame for the entire action with a tight shot. Additionally, the area of interest will, therefore, be less grainy.

Nevertheless, a normal lens (about 50mm for a 35mm camera) is basically all you need to get pictures that will sell to a newspaper.

As for speed, if you are a fair distance away from your subject—that is, if firemen, walking or moving normally in any way, are about a third to a half the height of the scene in your viewfinder frame—a good speed to catch the action is about 1/125 second. But if they are running, or if they are close up in your viewer—that is, the full height of your

A six-hour fire destroyed this local furniture store and warehouse. When I arrived at the scene shortly after the first alarm, most of the action was happening behind the building. I, as well as a few other photographers, took pictures there until the heat began to become intense and we were finally asked by firemen to move.

I went around to the front of the building—across the street—and just as I got there, the glass windows burst and flames poured out. A great deal of activity began to take place before me. The setting was ideal for photos. So I stationed myself with my viewfinder fixed on the fire truck on the left and the flaming building behind it. Whenever dramatic action took place in front of me, as on a stage, I took a shot of it.

I sold this picture to a wire service. The next day it appeared in newspapers across the state—and possibly elsewhere. I picked up several area newspapers to find it on the front page, and people later told me of its appearance in other newspapers that I never got to see.

Although I own the negative, I share ownership of the picture's use. A rubber-stamped notice on the back of the check I later received for it states that the wire service has the right to reuse the picture for no additional payment.

framed view or even larger—set your speed for about 1/250 second.

Just because a building is burning and firemen are hosing it down doesn't mean that a camera aimed in that direction and snapped will give you the emotional impact of the action that you may feel as an onlooker. If you just shoot blindly, you will discover when the photos are developed that you have very dull results. Firemen do their jobs routinely, and some even take bored stances. And that's exactly how they will show up in your pictures if you snap your shutter without thought.

On your arrival at a fire scene, survey the setting swiftly to determine the best vantage point for your camera. If there is fire, smoke, or both, you will want to capture that—but you will also want to include firemen, if possible, to provide the human element.

Go to various spots and look at the burning building, picturing the event as an already published newspaper photo. The viewfinder of your camera will be helpful in selecting the best composition by trial and error.

Shots taken from a low viewpoint, looking up at the fire— with firemen in front of you at work with hoses in the foreground—can give you dramatic pictures. Sometimes two or more firemen will be holding the same hose, and an artistic and dynamic composition can be obtained.

Always keep out of the way of those working so that your presence doesn't interfere with their important activities.

If you have a telephoto lens, focus it on parts of the building that are burning—where there are firemen. Be sure not to snap the shutter until firemen in your viewfinder are doing something meaningful, such as hosing through a window, tearing off a smoldering part of an eave, or engaging in any other kind of definite fire fighting task. If you just take pictures of whatever is in front of you without waiting for some kind of action, your photos will have less sale value than if you wait for the right moments. However, you might be able to sell unexciting pictures of a tragic fire in which someone died or was injured if your photos are the only ones available.

Another advantage automatically offered by a telephoto lens, whether it has a fixed focal length (for example, 135mm), or is a zoom (with a range such as 80mm to 200mm), is that a shot taken up at a window from the ground will give you a dramatic angle.

Clouds of smoke as well as flames are always dramatic on film; however, smoke must be photographed from certain relative positions or your pictures will be unsuccessful. If the wind is blowing the smoke toward you, making a screen between you and your subject, you will still be able to see firemen through it—though hazily. However, keep in mind that you, unlike a camera, can see the smoke moving. You will see some parts of the firemen and background at one moment, and then, at the next, those areas will be obscured and others will be revealed. What you observe may even appear to be interesting, perhaps even exciting. But for a still photograph, this is deceiving. When you snap your shutter you will record only one instant—and in that moment you will etch onto the film only patches of the firemen and background. Although in the darkroom it is possible to burn in from the negative in order to darken the smoke, the negative will have no firemen behind the smoke on the emulsion. Finally, a picture like this, when screened into dots for a newspaper, will lose even more quality; what little of the scene exists on the actual print will then be almost totally lost.

To avoid this problem caused by smoke, be sure to get on the side of the fire scene from which the wind is blowing. Then, when you shoot your picture, the smoke will be drifting away from you and whatever you are photographing.

There are, of course, other pictures that you can take than just the actual center of activity of a fire—which is, naturally, always the most important action to cover. There are often side issues that make for interesting photos. These kinds of shots sometimes turn out to be even more interesting than the main scene; or they may be supplementary, like a second photo to be published on the same incident.

Sometimes a hose setup with firemen just wetting down a

A

What you see is what you get. Just because drama is taking place before your lens doesn't mean that you can snap your shutter at any time to capture it. There are many times that subjects at a scene, such as the one shown, do not strike attitudes that represent the news event well.

You should always wait until there is animation—a gesture, an expressive posture, any action that conveys the mood and meaning of the

B

incident you are covering.

At fires, for example, there are many times that firemen may seem casual in their duties and not provide interesting shots, as the two men shown here looking off (A). But moments later (B), these same subjects can give you a good, saleable shot.

part of a burning building might give you an excellent shot, especially if it shows tension.

There are times that the victims of the fire are watching the fire fighting. If you can learn who they are for identification purposes, a newspaper might be interested in pictures of them showing an emotional reaction. Of course, whether you might want to take a picture like this depends on your own feelings. Or there might also be some resistance or anger by the subjects.

Many times, the local first aid squad is called to a scene to stand by. Occasionally, they have to give a soot-covered fireman a breath of oxygen. This is always a good newspaper shot.

Often an animal will be saved. Pet owners identify with such pictures, as well as nonowners and children, and editors like this kind of related picture if it is photographed well.

Once in a while there are victims being helped or carried on stretchers by emergency workers. If you can get a good action shot of this kind of incident, it is definitely a potential photo sale. For pictures such as these, close-ups are best, and they should be taken at about 1/250 second; farther back, 1/125 second will do.

How many pictures should you take? You, as the photographer, will be the best judge of that—probably. If you feel that you got one or two spectacular shots, odds are that you have what you need. However, even the professional press photographer is often fooled. Sometimes after the pictures are developed it turns out that what was thought to be an excellent shot isn't, and one thought to have been unexceptional turns out to be ideal. You are dealing in unknowns with press photography. Chance plays a major role; your guess can be as good as a pro's—or as bad.

Many times, the better opportunities for pictures come as the action gets under way. Sometimes, actual flames don't break out until long after the firemen arrive. Or the majority of firemen and other emergency people there first are not fully at work on the fire itself but are just getting ready to do their jobs.

Sometimes, when you look for the human element, it may be discovered to be other than human. Here are two kittens who were rescued from a hotel fire that I covered. An unexpected pictorial angle like this can give a newspaper reader a heartwarming moment, momentary relief from the usual words and pictures of the world's problems.

Being that spot-news events are unpredictable, you have to be constantly alert at a news scene. Skill and photographic knowledge are required. But so is luck.

It makes sense to shoot your entire roll of film, unless absolutely nothing more in photographable action is anticipated. It would only be a waste of valuable time for you to stand around finishing up your film when you should be on your way to a newspaper office.

But if there is a possibility of more action, and you have the time, you might as well stick around. The roll will have to be developed immediately, anyway. So, essentially, by finishing it up, you can use free film. Besides, sometimes the very last picture taken turns out to be the one the editor wants.

Structural fires (of houses, stores, garages, and other buildings) are not the only ones that occur. There are also fires involving cars, vans, trucks, boats, autumn leaves (uncontrolled), woods (brush), high tension wires, poles, and numerous other objects that can go up in flames. Each requires quick observation of the scene by the photographer preliminary to decisions about the best vantage points for taking pictures.

Vehicle fires occur at residences, parking lots, gas stations, and other places, but they also happen on roads.

Certain toll highways have rules that are not posted that forbid vehicles from stopping except for emergency purposes. If you do pull over to take a vehicle fire photo on such a road and are asked by a policeman to leave, it is best that you do so. If you refuse, you might be arrested—even if you are employed as a full-time newspaper photographer. Although you can stand up for your rights in court when your case comes up, it may not be worth the aggravation just on the possibility of making a photo sale—which may not even pan out. An employed press photographer choosing to defy the law is backed by a newspaper with its lawyers defending the right of freedom of the press. A freelancer isn't. And newspapers don't always win cases, either.

In most instances of vehicle fires, you should have no problems parking safely off the road or on a side street.

When you reach a vehicle fire scene that you will be photographing, evaluate the situation by moving around the subject as much as possible to find the best viewpoint—as you should with all on-the-spot news photos.

Shoot your pictures from an angle that gives you a recognizable vehicle, or whatever part of it is burning. If you can show flames or smoke, fine. A person using a fire extinguisher on the vehicle will add drama. Anyone involved in the action should be included in the picture.

As in photographing structural fires, be certain that no smoke obscures your view. It will only produce a hazy subject.

In most cases of vehicle fires, it is likely that you will arrive after the fire is out because firemen act quickly. Yet there may still be smoke, and even if there isn't, with enough damage to a vehicle your picture can still be saleable, provided it depicts the damage well. While you are aiming your camera to compose this shot, ask yourself if the picture you are about to snap would catch your own eye on a newspaper page.

At each fire there is usually one position that seems to offer the best angle. However, if there are vantage points that could be second-best, take advantage of them, too, while you can. If you hesitate, that moment will forever pass into the unphotographable past—and that opportunity may have given you a better shot than any you have.

The grab shot should also be considered, especially when you first arrive at a scene. A grab shot, as previously noted, is an almost blind, general photo—insurance that you will have *something*. If you don't manage to get anything else, you will at least have that.

Always consider the possibility of locating an elevated vantage point from a nearby structure. This can always give the newspaper reader an unusual view. Across the street or up the block there might be a tall building or a home with a second or third floor overlooking the blaze, or possibly a bridge.

It will cost you nothing to ask permission to photograph from the upper story of a residence or office building at the scene; at worst, you will be turned down. However, you will find that most people will be delighted to help you. When you tell them that you are taking press photos, they will already be thinking about clipping your picture from their newspaper and telling their friends about the experience they had when the photographer took that shot.

Often a newspaper that is unable to obtain an action shot of a fire will be satisfied with an aftermath picture, especially if it shows damage to a well-known site that is familiar to its readers, or when the incident was a tragic occurrence. If you can get to the scene while firemen are still there, or a fire inspector is examining the damage, you can still obtain interesting, saleable photos.

Auto Accident Photos

In Chapter 1 you were given a general idea of how to take pictures at an auto accident. Here are some finer details.

The newspaper reader is interested in seeing a picture that shows the victim of an accident. Of course, obtaining this is not always possible. Injured persons are rushed by ambulance to the hospital as soon as possible. And the photographer cannot always be there on the spot.

Showing damage is second choice.

If you arrive at a scene early enough, it is possible to photograph both the victim and damage.

A fixed-focus or medium zoom lens ranging between 35mm and 150mm is ideal for photographing the results of automobile accidents. Also, a wide-angle lens of 20mm to 35mm can be useful if you are able to move in extremely close, because the victim can be shown large, surrounded by emergency vehicles, apparatus, and emergency personnel.

Every situation is different and must be handled individually, depending on constantly changing circumstances. You should, when taking pictures, move in and out of the area of activity and at the same time keep totally out of the way of police and first aid people.

At typical auto accidents where the victim is removed from the car by first aid people, a certain procedure is usually followed. The victim is first treated for superficial injuries while still in the car, then is removed—usually on a backboard—to a stretcher waiting near the car. The stretcher is then wheeled to the ambulance and the victim carried inside and taken to the hospital.

Sometimes the source of light is such that the victim can be photographed through the front window of the car while being treated—provided no persons are in the way.

When taking traffic accident pictures, you must think and act quickly. Emergency people work fast in removing victims to the hospital, and the scene is quickly cleaned up by local wreckers because of the potential traffic hazard.

The best time for obtaining action shots is when the victim is being moved between the car and the ambulance. A shutter speed of 1/125 second to 1/250 second, depending on your proximity or the zoom-in view—and the speed of subject movement—should be satisfactory.

Be aware of light direction. Often, you will be facing the sun and will have to use a sunshade (a permanent, collapsible rubber one is best) and set your exposure by aiming the camera at a shadowed area of the ground first to make adjustments.

Standing somewhat away from the action, you can usually capture an overall dramatic scene.

It is usually best to show people in a photograph. However, there are times when a scene has so much impact by itself that it stands alone. Here are two examples, both of which I sold to a regional newspaper. The driver in the car-pole accident escaped injury, the newspaper reported. No one was in the car that went up in flames at a gas station.

Sometimes, extrication equipment must be used for a person trapped in a car. In such a case, try, if possible, to catch details of what mechanical activity is actually being done, rather than the backs of people blocking out what is taking place.

If passersby observing the scene are standing in your way, give them a tap and politely ask if they would temporarily move aside so that you can take pictures. They will usually do so.

Dealing with Police and Other Authorities at the News Scene

Although it is generally recognized by the press that it is absolutely within your rights to take pictures on a public street, if a person of authority tells you otherwise, it is best to handle the situation with diplomacy. Such disagreements are arbitrated regularly before judges.

First of all, a policeman may be looking out for your safety in an area where, for example, high voltage wires have fallen or a building on fire is in danger of collapse. Although the hazards in these situations might make getting photos even more desirable, you should not take the risks lightly.

In addition, you might consider it your right to take certain pictures, then learn that local authorities do not agree. Newspapers are in a position to protect their staffers with their lawyers. However, as a freelancer, you do not have that advantage. Nevertheless, there should be an American Civil Liberties Union branch in your area, as well as local, regional, and national representatives of professional photography organizations that can offer you advice as a member. However, keep in mind that they will not necessarily defend you.

Should you encounter such a resistant situation, politeness, common sense, and patience should ensure admission to the scene. Sometimes all that is required is some waiting. Other times you might not be successful in getting exactly the picture you want; yet, a compromise photo might be obtained that will fill the bill.

The more you cover spot-news events in your area, the better the chances that you will be recognized as a familiar press photographer by local authorities and allowed to take your pictures without interference.

Press Cards

If you frequently submit photos to area newspapers, they might issue you a press card if you ask for one. After all, it is to their advantage to have their area well covered.

Some photography organizations provide press cards to members.

Often, though, if you just state to an official, when asked, that you are a press photographer, you will be allowed to take pictures. In most cases, in fact, you will find that policemen, firemen, and other officials are not only cooperative but helpful in providing you with information to aid you in your picture taking and in gathering caption data.

A Different Viewpoint: Aerial Photography

It is quite possible that you may receive an assignment to shoot pictures for a newspaper from an airplane, or you may decide to do so on your own. Many kinds of pictures taken from the air can be of use to an editor. An extraordinary fire with smoke visible for many miles especially interests readers when it also shows the site of the disaster within a familiar area. Aerial viewpoints of such scenes as a boat in trouble on the water or a topographical view of a location that will soon have more buildings, or on which new construction has just been completed, also draw a newspaper reader's interst.

If you have an airport near you that rents planes and provides pilots, you can usually pay for this service on a part-of-an-hour basis.

Single-engine planes sometimes have windows that can be opened. Helicopters, which cost more to rent, are usually used by the photographer with a door removed

Standard film with the use of a haze filter developed in regularly used developer should give you satisfactory results. If you wish to go beyond this basic level, there are special films and developers available that are designed to deal with this kind of photography with more sophistication.

One morning two automobile accident calls on different frequencies came over my scanner within seconds of each other. I went to the one that reported that people were trapped. I arrived at the tragic scene almost 25 minutes later. Three people had died: a mother and her two children. Their car had skidded, collided with a van, and caught fire. A truck driver and two other men passing by had managed to pull the woman from the burning vehicle, and she and one child had already been taken to the hospital.

I stood by, much affected by the grim scene, as I watched the emergency workers cut their way through metal to extricate the body of the third victim. The picture I took just after the removal was accepted by one of my area newspapers and appeared on their front page; the other, showing the extrication, was printed on the inside, where the article was continued.

Feelings of Guilt: Photographing Others' Misfortunes

The professional press photographer is a person who cares about people. That is what journalism—and photojournalism—are all about: recording for history the drama of mankind. For that reason the photographer is often affected by the scene in the camera viewfinder—and sometimes finds it very painful to snap. An accident victim in pain, a body being carried out of a burned building—incidents such as these often cause the photographer to ask himself: Is this how I'm making my living? Am I so callous that I can earn income by taking pictures of human tragedy?

As simple as the answer to this question seems, it is nevertheless true: whether or not you took the pictures, the event would have happened. And in most cases, the publication of such photos serves not only to inform the public about what can affect people's lives, but also as a potential preventive measure for the reader.

There are many occasions when newspaper editors must seriously consider and debate whether it would be proper journalism to publish a specific picture. Sometimes, in fact, when a newspaper does print a borderline photo, it receives strong feedback through letters from readers.

In the final analysis, if there is a question as to whether a picture should be taken, you as a photojournalist must use your own reason, taste, logic, and moral outlook. If the result is affirmative, it is then up to your editor whether the photo is finally published.

Keeping Informed of News Events

The Scanner—Police, Fire, and First Aid Radio

If you intend to devote time and effort to freelance press photography, you may want to consider buying a scanner. If you are in an area where there are only a couple of frequencies broadcasting this emergency information, you may be able to pick it up on a radio with short-wave capability. However, if you reside near a number of towns or in a metropolitan area, you will want to have as complete radio coverage as possible.

Scanners range from the simple crystal type, which gives you one to several frequencies, to the programmable kind, which will scan through frequencies currently on the airways or stop at specific ones at the push of a button.

Police, fire, and first aid personnel use codes on these radio bands in order to convey quickly the type of emergency involved and to be certain that the messages are understood clearly. These codes are also generally not known to most of the public, and certain areas use specific codes not in use elsewhere.

One time, an announcement came over my scanner: a truck had overturned. The incident had happened within a fifteen-minute drive of my home. I went there immediately. After I had parked and was rushing to the scene with my camera in hand I saw—in the distance—that the local first aid squad was already putting the truck driver into an ambulance. It was too late to get a shot of the victim against the background of the upset truck.

The aftermath was all that was left to be recorded; yet, there was much to photograph. The truck, which had been carrying sand, had landed on its side on the front lawn of a home and spilled its contents across the grass. In order to condense as much of the scene as possible, I used my wide-angle lens and shot from every point possible that would tell the story of what had happened.

When I was about to leave, a woman approached me and told me she worked for an area newspaper and asked if my pictures were for sale. I explained that before I could sell any I would first have to get an okay from the editor of a local tabloid for which I was covering such happenings.

If you offer pictures of an incident to more than one newspaper, it is not only an ethical practice, but good business—and good sense—to ask each if it is all right to offer other frames from your negatives elsewhere, as well as to mention any sales made. You want your intentions to be

crystal clear and understood so that no one feels you have been underhanded. It's not just a matter of avoiding hurting any feelings or preventing subsequent anger—you also want to sell again to these markets.

Usually, if you ask if it is all right to sell elsewhere, the answer will be affirmative, especially if you have such a variety of angles that none are alike. Editors of newspapers, large and small, understand that a photographer doesn't come across news items every day, that this is how a freelance photojournalist earns a living.

Should you find that you don't have a broad choice of pictures of a single happening, you can sometimes provide an entirely different-looking second photo by cropping or enlarging a limited area of a full shot similar to the first choice.

If you sell to a wire service, don't offer the photo to a newspaper that uses that service and that will, therefore, get the same photo off the wire later in the day.

Your own situation will dictate where to offer your first choice. It might be the newspaper that pays best, gives you the most assignments, or has the most prestige. You might even have an arrangement in your area with a number of newspapers that you will offer all of them spot-news photos of any event you cover. If so, this will keep you on your toes in finding varying viewpoints when taking pictures.

In the situation of the overturned truck, my first-choice editor made a selection and didn't object to my selling a photo elsewhere. The other editor, who called me on the phone as a result of my meeting his employee at the scene of the accident, just asked for a good print. I selected one for him that was quite different from the first one accepted—as you can see here. The shot the preferred editor chose shows the front of the truck; the other shows the underside.

Your local newspaper editor will be able to give you a list of your area's codes, or you might be able to obtain them from the police or other emergency groups.

If you listen often to your scanner, the constant use of the commonly used codes and the circumstances under which they are used will eventually suggest their meanings.

The scanner often will have you on a nearby news scene

before firemen or first aid people appear. This is an advantage you will have over nearby metropolitan newspaper staff competition. Although editors hear these radio calls, they do not have the photography personnel to dispatch constantly over a broad area. Even when photographers are available, editors are not always able to get them to a news scene quickly. Sometimes a call that may sound routine, and which an editor may choose to ignore for that reason, turns out to be one of importance that can provide a photographer with startling pictures.

Nuclear Plant. One man died and three were injured in this column collapse at a nuclear plant being built in Forked River–Oyster Creek, New Jersey. I heard a first aid call, then additional calls for aid from surrounding communities. It was a long trip for me, about forty-five minutes. Naturally, by the time I arrived the victims had been taken off in ambulances. I used a zoom lens (43–86mm) so that I could move in and out and compose this shot to obtain the dramatic effect I wanted. I sold it to *The New York Times*.

Scanners that can be installed in a car are available. In addition, there are battery-operated scanners that can be hand-held. Certain localities, however, do not permit the use of a scanner in a car. In such situations, it may be necessary to obtain written permission from the police chief of the area in which you will be taking pictures. Sometimes, a letter from your local police chief will suffice for all surrounding areas. Therefore, if you would like to use your scanner on the road, you should look into this matter in the areas you intend to cover.

Your Local Radio Station

Always listen to local radio, especially early in the morning when you can learn about what happened overnight. Fires and other happenings that took place after the last evening's deadlines are news for two days following and can be covered without rush or tension. Aftermath pictures are often of great interest to newspaper editors. Fires, for example, that at the start—and at dusk, with flash—might have produced pictures only of firemen and smoke can later show extensive damage, which is more meaningful to the newspaper reader who is familiar with the scene before the incident (unless, of course, those early shots can show exciting action). In addition, if an early morning news event is still happening after sunrise, you will be able to cover it when you are fully informed of the details, because reporters will have dug up facts all night.

Your Newspapers

Yes, the newspapers of your area can, themselves, bring you sales. Read them in detail to keep up on coming events—book sales, bazaars, civic events, strikes, and other planned happenings. You might note these in a diary. When you have the time, you can then cover what is happening at that moment and afterward call the editor, who may want to look at your pictures. The editor might not have thought that the event would produce interesting pictures or was just unable to have it covered. Perhaps you might be able to show, with your results, that it was worth covering after all.

15

Sports Photography

Local tabloids and regional and metropolitan newspapers cover high school sports. It is often in this area of newspaper photography that freelancers are given many assignments.

Shutter speeds required for various sports differ, and depth of field should always be considered. Refer to Chapter 5 for details on these elements of photography.

You may want to experiment with speeds for athletics. Generally, though, average shutter settings for certain sports should be followed: baseball, football, and soccer—1/125 to 1/500 second; tennis—1/500 to 1/1000 second; and speedboat racing—1/500 to 1/2000 second.

These speeds, of course, depend on factors such as your proximity to the subject, the size of the subject in the viewfinder, and the direction that a person or object is moving with relation to the camera. Movement toward or away from the camera requires less shutter speed than it does from side to side.

Newspapers require identification of at least the major subjects of sports pictures. This is usually a simple task, accomplished by matching the number worn by a player with a list of players. But there can be problems if a number on a jersey cannot be read.

It is best to arrive at the playing field before the game so that you can obtain the names and numbers of the players. If there is little time or opportunity to copy the list, you can use an expedient method commonly employed by sports photographers. Just obtain from the coach or person in charge of each team the list of players and their numbers, put it on a bench or the ground, and snap a close-up picture of it. A commonly used 50mm lens will do the trick; if you want to get very close, buy yourself an inexpensive close-up lens that you can screw onto your regular lens. Then, after you process your film, you can either make an enlargement of the list or read the negative with a loupe—the special magnifying lens for such use that is available at camera supply stores.

Don't, however, rely totally on identifying the action people in your shots immediately after the film is developed from their numbers in the pictures. You may have taken a spectacular shot, yet the person of primary interest in it may not be identifiable by number because he or she is turned the wrong way or the jersey number is blocked by another player.

When you take a picture, immediately make a note of the name and/or number of the main athlete, matching it up with the action by a description—of one to a few words—of what activity you recorded on film and the team that person is on. As a double-check against uniform colors, shades in black and white should also be in your notes: "Team A—dark jerseys; light bottoms with dark stripes," etc. You can nail down your record by matching that shot with the manufacturer's sequence numbers on the film's sprocketed edge as compared to the numbers in the frame counter window of your camera. Further accuracy can be ensured by shooting a blank frame now and then and entering it in your notes as a marker between groups of shots.

A sports photographer working against a deadline often has little time to spend at a game before rushing off to the darkroom to start developing the film for the next day's edition. Newspaper pictures, in fact, usually have to be taken during about the first fifteen minutes or so of a game.

Certain basic lenses and techniques are used for various sports. Beyond this, however, each photographer must discover by trial and error what equipment and methods of working are most individually productive.

In sports, probably more than in most other phases of press photography, the photojournalist is at the mercy of chance.

Regarding choices of lenses, here are a few general suggestions to begin with; you can then modify them to suit your needs.

In football, soccer, and other sports similar in their presentation of players to the photographer, a range of focal lengths from about 50mm to 200mm, either fixed-focus or zoom, will provide the views necessary for photographing these sports. They will fill your frame nicely from a sideline position of about ten feet from the action to middle-of-the-field players.

Focusing can be handled in either of two ways. You can focus in the zone where the action is expected to take place, or you can follow a major player, focusing simultaneously. One-touch zoom lenses can be focused on a player and left at that setting, requiring only the need to move the view in and out—with that player remaining in focus.

Sometimes a sequential series of shots taken with a motor drive, auto winder, or just quick reflexes can be helpful in more than one way. Besides giving you a good selection of frames of action from which to select (or, perhaps a series of pictures for use), it provides the opportunity of identifying players whose numbers are not visible in a picture that the editor might want to use—through prior or subsequent shots in which their numbers are recognizable.

Games such as tennis can require faster shutter speeds and focal lengths of 200mm or higher to achieve an effect you might desire of a telescoped or compressed subject and an unblurred ball, depending, of course, on your distance from the subject.

The Conquerers. I was sent on an assignment by a local paper to a soccer finals game. I was told that if the home team won, the sports editors would like—in addition to the action game shots—a photo of triumph, possibly of one of the players being carried on the shoulders of his teammates. The team did win and, after the clock ran out, the muddied players grasped each other in victorious celebration and simply ran off the field. As they did, I went toward them and got this and other pictures. I continued shooting the winners as they were given a standard presentation of a trophy, and I took pictures as one member held the trophy high and ran around the field with the others following. But I'd already had the necessary photo of triumph in the bag, as I discovered when I looked at the developed negatives. Two shots I had taken during the game were run in the sports section. This one ended up on the front page.

Sports. A photographer should always look for the unusual while still getting the regular shots. That applies to sports, too. I was taking the ordinary sliding-into-base pictures at a high school baseball game that I was assigned to cover freelance, when a player at first base tried to steal second. But he found himself trapped as the first and second basemen threw the ball back and forth until they tagged him out. I was at home plate—a long distance from the action—but I had my 80mm–200mm telephoto lens on my camera. So I set it on the fullest long focus—200mm—and shot this picture. Even then, I still had to enlarge the negative considerably to crop out the extraneous scenery. But of the five photos of the game that I turned in, this one was published in the sports section the next day.

Baseball pictures can be taken from a number of positions. Your choice will usually depend on the status of the game at any given moment. A player on first base may put you between home plate and first base; a player on third base might have you between there and home plate. From each of these positions, using a 100mm to 200mm zoom lens, you can also cover third base—if your reaction time is fast enough.

Indoor sports activity, such as basketball, does not require lenses of long focal lengths—50mm to 100mm is usually sufficient. However, a wide aperture—though it requires exact focusing—can be an advantage if you shoot under available light.

If a gymnasium where basketball is being played is poorly lit, flash will probably be necessary. This, unfortunately, produces heavy shadows and dark backgrounds. However, if conditions are such that you can push-process, you will have the advantage of working under dramatic lighting. Usually, you can obtain good push-process results by raising an ASA 400 film rating to 1000. Contrast might be a little too high at 1600, 2000, or 3200—but then, it might not be. It all depends on the sources of light at the game scene.

When taking your reading for push-processing, do not look through your viewfinder at highly reflective surfaces or objects. To determine your exposure, find an average view for your meter reading that is typical of the ball game shots you will be taking.

When going to a ball game on assignment, always confirm the time, place, and teams playing. Sometimes the information reaching the editor giving out the assignment is not accurate. Try to obtain the phone numbers of the athletic department or administrative offices of the competing schools. Call them and ask about these facts as well as when the game is to begin and whether there is to be any activity before them, such as marching bands or other demonstrations.

Sports photography is a constant challenge. Sometimes you can't be sure of what you have until you examine it on film. Many times you will come up with just an average picture when you thought you had captured an exciting instant. Other times, you will find—to your great satisfaction—that what you had expected would be a typical shot turns out to be a peak moment.

16

The Feature Picture

One of the most common types of newspaper assignments for the freelance press photographer is feature photography. A major service that a newspaper provides for its readers is the feature article that tells about local people, various activities going on, and other situations of interest in the area of distribution of the publication's circulation. It may deal with politics, art, schools, or any other of an unlimited range of subjects.

The newspaper staffer giving you the assignment—usually an editor or someone in charge of a department—will present it to you either written up on a form or by phone. The work- or job-order, filled out by a reporter and authorized by an editor, has general information about the text that the photographer is to illustrate. It includes descriptions of suggested photos and provides phone numbers of contacts or people who are mentioned in or associated with the story. The contact will usually be in a position to provide you with detailed information or entree to the feature setting or event, perhaps meeting you there and introducing you to the people

Feature photo sales possibilities are all around you. Keep a calendar of annual area activities. Then go to these events early, shoot on spec, call your surrounding newspapers, and tell them what you have.

This is one of many pictures I took at a county fair. I sold it the same day.

you will be photographing or taking you on a tour of an area to be photographed.

However, there will be times when, due to the fact that there is little information to go on at the start of an article, you will have to be resourceful. Just as a reporter would have to uncover facts, you will have to dig up ways and means to attain your photographic goals.

Occasionally, the finished story is provided in printout or

typed form. If this is the case, you should read the piece, which can suggest ideas to you that complement the ones provided by the newspaper.

Always call the contact immediately after receiving the assignment. Often, time is of the essence with regard to people being available at any given time, and you will want to set up a meeting as soon as possible.

Get directions for getting to your assignment from the contact or the name and number of someone to whom you can be referred for the information. Also, ask questions about the situation you will be photographing. Your contact may assume that you know all the details, since they may have given such information to the reporter or editor. Explain that, as a photographer, you were given only the bare details, and that by being informed about the subject, you will be able to come up with picture ideas that will more fully illustrate the story. Using these new facts, you can plan additional, possibly more creative, shots than you might have thought of earlier.

The availability of space when the page on a particular story is made up will determine the number and size of your photographs to be used for the piece. Although this may have been predetermined, you should nevertheless cover every possibility that might be considered for the layout. Interesting pictures might change an editor's outlook on the size of a display. Your ideas might even include some photographs that the reporter and editor had not thought of or noted but that suggest themselves after you look over the setting. Consider angles looking up, angles looking down, tight shots, and wide-angle shots. Think about how you might light each scene, with either available illumination or supplementary sources, to create effects that will give the person making up the page meaty photos that, when cropped and juxtaposed, can be fashioned into a dynamic words-and-picture layout.

A principal character in the foreground against a background that represents the essence of the story is often effective.

When taking pictures of persons head on, do editors prefer that the subject look at the camera or away? Outlooks on this

Location Filming. When the movie *Rocky II* was being shot in Philadelphia, reasonably near where I live, I drove there to do a story and interview with pictures on speculation. I got a lot of good shots of the filming itself, but the most interesting and human photo turned out to be one I took during a break. The star-director, Sylvester Stallone, posed while one of the local kids, who played a bit part in the film, took his picture. It was one of the three pictures the newspaper used with my article.

point vary from editor to editor. Sometimes a direct stare out of the newspaper page at the reader creates a striking effect. Other times, a line of vision by the subject that is askew to the camera's can capture the essence of that person's personality.

Therefore, once the subject is in the position you desire, with the lighting you want, you might ask that person to look at you for one or more shots, then slightly away for others. That either satisfies an editor's preference or provides a choice of what turns out to look best.

When taking feature photos of people, the subject or subjects often have to be posed. There are many ways of doing this so that the activity depicted seems to be spontaneous. People who are portrayed doing some form of action can be posed in that manner, usually with their eyes directed appropriately. This can in some cases, however, cause their eyes to appear closed. To overcome this problem, simply ask them to look up and off into the distance, or shoot your picture from a low point.

Another way to obtain a feeling of spontaneity in your photographs is first to have the subjects pose as you set the camera; then have them actually work at what they are doing while you click off moments that catch them in action.

Interesting compositions can be obtained with groups of people by placing one or more in the foreground.

When identifying a group shot, depending on the number of people in it, provide the editor with the names of all the subjects, if possible; if not, give at least the names of the principals.

One identifying picture to start, with everyone lined up and identified from left to right, will leave you free to shift people around without further notes.

Should you be taking pictures of a number of people, all of whom are important, it is usually best to take a few sequential shots. Once in a while your main subject or one person in a group will have his or her eyes closed, and you won't discover it until the film comes out of the wash. I once took a quick series of similar poses, from slightly different angles, of a single subject whose eyes were closed on every one of the five frames. However, I also had other shots of that subject with open eyes.

When shooting spontaneous movement of people within a

setting, you will often find that one of a series has just that magical touch of composition that none of the others has.

Many times, when you are on assignment, your subject or a contact will request certain poses. You may not agree with their concept, and you may be certain that the editor wouldn't, either. Nevertheless, in such circumstances it is usually best for the subject-photographer-newspaper relationship to satisfy their requests, then go on with your own ideas. Sometimes, in fact, asking your subject about what else there is to photograph regarding the article can bring suggestions that will be of benefit.

Is it ever improper to pose a newspaper shot? Common sense should dictate the answer to that question under whatever conditions you are shooting. Naturally, you are not going to create visual news by, for example, asking a policeman to stand in front of a bank and point his gun the way he did a half hour before when he caught a robber. But if you have the opportunity to pose him, and he is willing to cooperate, it would most fittingly convey his bravery and the incident if you had him holding his fists on his hips, looking off from the doorway of the bank. What you want to do in such a situation, then, is recreate a mood, symbolize an incident.

Head shots, or portraits, are always worthwhile to take in addition to your planned shots if the time and opportunity allow it. A newspaper can always use a fresh portrait of a person in the news for its library files. Space limitations might, in fact, become so tight by deadline time that a head shot could turn out to be the ideal picture for a story.

The head shot is a very commonly used type of newspaper picture. It is usually printed one column wide, sometimes a half-column wide.

Many kinds of lighting can be used for these portraits, which are sometimes also called head-and-shoulder pictures.

Head shots can be taken with flash, available light, floods, and spotlights, or a combination of these, to produce simple or complex artistic lighting. And in press photography you usually have to be prepared to set up your lighting quickly.

If you get together with the subject and find you both have a little extra time, you can use it to plan and arrange the lighting.

To start off with the simplest and quickest method, let's consider flash: your flashgun mounted on the camera, pointed directly at the subject. To improve on the flat lighting that this will produce, remove the flashgun from the camera and hold it high and to one side, pointing it precisely at the subject. Another choice is bounce light, using the same setup but aiming the flashgun at a reflective surface usually removed from the camera, such as the ceiling.

You can produce out-of-the-ordinary lighting, which might influence an editor to publish your picture larger than planned, by standing a subject by a window or in a doorway, either toward or away from the light, and using flash fill-in. For information on how to expose for this kind of illumination, refer to Chapter 7. For the head shot you would be closer to the subject either in footage or by means of a zoom or telephoto lens. A lens of 100 to 135mm is ideal for portraits without distortion and, with the setting's background slightly out of focus, for a feeling of mood.

The usual classical studio lighting can be achieved simply and easily with the use of two floodlights—one facing the subject and the other to the side, with a spotlight behind the head for highlighting. Many variations of this lighting can be found in books on basic photography.

It is very important to take backup shots as a precaution. Don't rely on one lighting setup. Then, in the event that the lighting of your first shots does not produce statisfactory results, you will have head shots with one or more additional kinds of lighting. If you shoot your initial pictures with flash, take a few with available light indoors, some outdoors, and some with a combination of natural light and flash. Sometimes such insurance can yield better pictures from the rushed or unplanned lighting because of its spontaneity.

The simple portrait snapped close up outside is usually a good solid backup.

This swearing in of Howard W. Kushner as Mayor of Island Heights, New Jersey, by his law partner, Hugh R. Riley, is the type of picture that can get you started in photojournalism. Local tabloids, and sometimes even area newspapers, don't always have the manpower to cover such scheduled news activities. Let your surrounding editors know that you are available to take pictures of civic and other events that occur where you live or nearby. This kind of photography might be your "foot in the door."

Certain news feature events occur with boring regularity. These are the awarding of plaques, the giving of checks, groundbreakings, groups of people standing around at parties for charities, monument unveilings, ribbon cuttings, the giving of the key to a city, speakers at microphones, and other trite scenes.

Such happenings are a challenge to the creative photographer to think of fresh and original scenes that can delight the reader's eye. Instead of people posing with shovels at a groundbreaking, you can show a couple of businessmen helping an architect carry a model of the finished building out of a car before the event. Instead of a check being handed to the administrator of a hospital, you can show the donor in the

One day I got a call from the editor of a neighborhood tabloid with a circulation of about 5,000. Former President Gerald R. Ford, he informed me, was going to be in town to visit a private school that Ford had attended. Although Ford was occasionally making news on various issues, this would be a quiet situation that would be of interest only to the local community. I agreed to cover the event.

I went there and, on Ford's arrival, got several shots of him being greeted at the school with a crowd of students behind him. Then I waited around until after he had finished dinner with the headmaster. By that time it was dusk. When he emerged from the headmaster's home, local children were waiting to obtain autographs. There was only a small group of people, and I was the only photographer. So it was with ease that I took pictures of the autographing in a calm atmosphere as relaxed secret service men looked on.

Notables do not have to be photographed at earth-shattering or even special events. I am certain that the people in this community were delighted to see pictures of what had occurred in their hometown: a former U.S. President had visited. Besides, it isn't often that we see pictures of public figures in moments when stress doesn't prevail.

On the technical side, the dusk shot of the autographing was taken with a fast film at its normal ASA 400, using an $f/1.2$ lens not quite at its fullest opening, which allowed me a reasonable, though low, speed. Had I used flash, I would not have had to worry about holding the camera extremely still, but I would have lost the mood created by the background—which would have been black. Also, with flash, the range of light gradation that modeled the faces and figures of the subjects would have been replaced by flat illumination.

There are many civic and other occasions that you can shoot on spec for a local newspaper. The public is notified of these events in advance. Here is a picture I took on Veterans Day at a bank less than a mile from my residence. I had also shot pictures of ceremonies at a nearby firehouse. Of the pictures I submitted, this one was bought.

Hollywood does a lot of location shooting—in cities and towns all over America and around the world. Keep your eyes and ears attuned to what's coming up. You'll get that information on the radio, from your local newspaper, and elsewhere. And it doesn't just have to be movies. TV commercials are show biz, too—and they are also filmed everywhere.

The first day of Woody Allen's location shooting of his motion picture *Stardust Memories* took place not far from where I live. When I arrived there, as I expected, personnel were discouraging the taking of pictures. Woody Allen, it is well known, is quite averse to publicity and news photographers. Still, camera people from local newspapers arrived on the scene, and since they were not allowed close to where the filming was to be done, telephoto lenses were put to work.

I took this picture with my 80mm–200mm zoom at its fullest extension, capturing a moment when Woody Allen, standing in the midst of his cast and crew members, studied his script.

A picture like this always has a good chance of finding an interested editor—and often more than once.

children's wing speaking with young patients. Instead of the giving of a key to the city, you can show the mayor and guest casually chatting against the area's familiar skyline.

For such news feature happenings, if the photographer arrives early, it is sometimes possible to get something different before the formal activities get under way. If nothing is going on at the start, officials are usually most cooperative and amenable to a photographer's ideas for poses.

Sometimes, just shooting pictures spontaneously at a civic occasion can bring you off-the-cuff dramatic pictures.

If you are taking feature pictures by means of available light and there is doubt about lighting and exposure, it is always good practice to take backup pictures with flash, if possible.

Signs are very important elements of feature pictures and should be included in your shooting whenever possible. Signs fix a time, place, or situation solidly for the newspaper reader. They can also add to the mood. Signs may be prominent, in the background, or slightly out of focus. Sometimes a sign, as a picture in itself, can have impact; on occasion, an editor may want to use one as an inset.

When photographing signs, always be careful about exposures. White or light-colored signs can give your exposure meter an incorrect reading. To set your exposure quickly and correctly, find a setting adjacent to the sign that is "average," such as trees and branches partially lit by sunlight, and use that to set aperture and speed for the sign.

In summary, feature photography provides the press photographer with probably the best opportunity in the total scope of photojournalism to be creative. Instead of being restricted to the limitations of an uncontrollable event, the photojournalist can, in most cases, actually have a hand in placement of the subjects, composition of the setting, and arrangement of the lighting.

17

The Photo Story/Photo Essay

Many newspapers publish features fully illustrated with photographs on various local subjects. They may be stories illustrated with photos, or they may be primarily photographic layouts—as total mood pieces—with captions being the only text. There are also some pieces that could be categorized as being in between these two extremes.

If your local tabloid or newspaper runs this type of photo page, or there is a chance that they would, put one or more together to submit. After all, the newspaper may never have done this because nothing of that sort was ever offered to the editor. Multiple photos of a single subject make an excellent showcase for your talents. You should find around you unlimited subjects that lend themselves to this kind of photo illustration. Shoot a roll or two of pictures on a local situation that interests you. Select from those negatives a wide range of views that give insight into the story from varying angles. You might very well have it accepted by your local editor on the spot.

These kinds of photo layouts give the press photographer an opportunity to be extremely creative, and they can very well help open doors for you in press photography—not only with that newspaper but with others, once you have work in print to show around.

In shooting your picture story, consider every aspect of the circumstances, which might involve a person, place, or situa-

Always keep an eye out for news pictures. The possibilities are all around you: an unusual billboard; a local reaction to a national situation; a monument or other representation that is symbolic for your area, the region, state, or country—many such situations wait to be photographed.

I was coming back from an assignment for a large metropolitan newspaper and pulled into a gas station on a toll road to have my tank filled. This was during the period that gas prices were rising at a considerable rate, and new pumps that could accommodate more digits were replacing the obsolete ones in current use.

As it turned out, I happened to arrive at this gas station just as many of the old pumps, which had been removed, were standing together waiting to be hauled away. My 24mm wide-angle lens took in the old and new pumps, the station, and a line of cars awaiting fueling. When I turned in my assignment, I included my film on the additional news situation. The newspaper bought this picture and published it with the heading: "Headstones in a Gas-Pump Graveyard." This sale was in addition to payment received for my regular—simultaneous—assignment.

tion. You might also go through photojournalism books and magazines featuring this type of photography at your local library to help spark ideas.

Use every conceivable type of lighting that you can think of; in each picture you take, attempt to capture the essence of what you are trying to say as an overall statement.

Along the lines of this type of endeavor, some newspapers publish "weather" photos. These pictures depict, usually with local people—singly, in juxtaposition, or in a montage—the type of day it is: blustery, rainy, cold, hot, sunny. Caption information usually gives the names of the subjects, what is happening, a brief description of the day's weather, and an upcoming forecast.

Many daily newspapers publish "weather" pictures—or might. And biweekly and weekly tabloids occasionally print pictures of heavy snows, flooding, and the like. Always be aware of unseasonable turns in the weather. And don't overlook seasonal ones, either. There are unlimited possibilities for subjects and scenes depicting a weather situation—with children, adults, animals, crowds, or objects.

This is a picture I took at a frozen lake about five miles from where I live. I submitted it on spec to a large-circulation newspaper whose area of distribution includes my township. They bought it and published it the next day with the heading: "Conjuring Up Currier & Ives."

18

Spot News

Selling Spot News by Phone

Once you establish relationships with newspapers and wire service bureaus, and the editors there are familiar with your work and confident that you can turn in at least a competent news photo every time, you will usually be able to make a sale with a phone call. In fact, after regular sales, those phone calls will most likely—by invitation of the editor—be made collect.

You will usually be able to reach someone by phone at the average metropolitan daily almost any time except the wee hours of the morning. The newsroom begins to come alive after 8:00 A.M. And, before noon, activity is usually humming. Depending upon staff schedules, a person who is authorized to purchase freelance photographs should show up sometime between 9:00 and 11:00 A.M.

Once you reach the editor who can buy your work, give details about the incident you covered, but make them as brief and concise as possible. Editors are busy people who follow

When extraordinarily adverse weather strikes, newspapers that buy from freelancers are interested in obtaining unusual pictures: trees fallen on highways, flooding, jackknifed trucks, cars trapped in snow, and even the brighter side—children sledding. This picture is of a nearby creek that overflowed during heavy rains that covered a great surrounding area. I sold it to a large-circulation newspaper.

exacting schedules and are often inundated with news copy and pictures from which they must make selections for limited space. Describe as accurately as possible the pictures you took.

The editor may already be aware of the news event you photographed. Word of it might have come in over the wire, through a phone tip, or via one of the newspaper reporters who keeps in touch with authorities in that area—perhaps at the newspaper's bureau near you.

In most instances you should be able to obtain an instant decision as to whether the newspaper will consider purchasing your pictures of the event. Sometimes, however, though there is interest, the editor must check with other staff members to determine whether the newspaper has already covered the happening photographically and whether the incident is newsworthy enough for publication.

If you are invited to the newsroom, ask about the film processing situation before you hang up. Will you deliver finished prints or will they process your pictures? In time, of course, with regular sales to editors, standard arrangements will be established.

Should you plan to offer your pictures to more than one market, be certain that each editor is fully cognizant of your intentions.

Deadlines for Spot News

Deadlines for morning papers vary, but the earlier in the day—say, by early afternoon—you can supply pictures, or at least let the editor know they are coming, the better chance you have of making a sale. As the day progresses, more and more copy and photographs become earmarked for page makeup, and toward evening the only pictures that have a chance of being accepted are those of stronger import than what is beginning to fill the pages.

Morning dailies are put to bed the evening before, from possibly a few hours before to just past midnight. Some newspapers print updated editions after their initial runs.

Sunday newspapers have many sections that are preprinted; that is, sections that are not on tight deadline, such as those for entertainment and real estate, magazines, and other such parts. These come off the presses toward the end of the preceding week and are delivered in advance to newsstands, stores, and other outlets.

News sections—aside from their advertising and feature-page portions—are kept open until the last moment for late-breaking news. However, because of the size of Sunday newspapers and the logistics of their delivery, Sunday newspaper news sections are often put onto the press earlier than the weekday editions. Therefore, if you are covering an incident on a Saturday, you may have an earlier deadline.

Sunday, it should be noted, is usually a wide-open day for freelance press photography sales. The newspaper staff often

This is a combination holiday and "weather" picture. It was taken on a Memorial Day weekend at one of many beaches in the circulation sales area of the large metropolitan newspaper that bought it.

On Sunday morning of the holiday weekend I scouted the resort area for interesting scenes. I also took pictures on the nearby boardwalks, where amusements and concession stands were similarly jammed with the first visitors of the season. After shooting the pictures, which was about noon, I called the newspaper—to which I had previously sold pictures—and asked if they would like to see the photos I had taken. I described the scenes. The answer was affirmative.

I brought my "raw" film to their photo lab, where it was developed and a photo editor selected a few frames. These were printed for the final choice. This picture, used to illustrate the area's beginning-of-the-summer activities, accompanied an article on the subject that began on page 1. It was one of a series of frames that I had clicked off, moving in and out with an 80mm–210mm lens. Special care had to be taken in metering this scene because the sunny beach was glaring. Sunday is usually a wide-open day for freelance picture sales.

gets going later than usual, and coverage is often not as intensive as it is during the week. Not much is happening on Sunday, either, contrary to weekdays, when the activity of daily living is high. And the next day, Monday, is when people will be picking up their newspapers early, after a restful weekend, to be informed and entertained at the start of the new work week. Sunday deadline is late, as it is on weekdays. So a news event picture to help fill the pages of an uneventful weekend will be welcomed by editors, who will listen interestedly when you call to report about what you have on film.

Sometimes a newspaper will give you a photo assignment at about noon for a news story that is being developed for the next day's edition. In such a case, they keep a hole open, realizing that the pictures will arrive somewhat late in the day.

My experience in obtaining this picture only confirms the fact that it pays to have your camera with you at all times. I spotted this car fire while on my way to a metropolitan newspaper to deliver finished prints of a news event (a school fire), which I had sold by phone. The newspaper developed the film and it resulted in a second sale. Both pictures appeared the next day. These pictures were accepted on a Sunday, which is usually wide open for freelance press photographers.

It's a good idea to inquire about, and make note of, deadline times for your area newspapers. But don't think about deadline times for photos of extremely important news events. If a news incident is strong enough, it will have follow-up coverage the next day—and, perhaps, past then— and photos that have missed the initial deadline will certainly interest editors.

Whether you are on assignment or delivering spot news as raw film or finished prints, you should always get your work to the newspaper as soon as possible. Even pictures for features that are scheduled for several days hence, or longer, cannot be received soon enough. Concrete planning for make-up can commence only when your pictures are in-house. And if the pictures you deliver are not exactly what was expected, the entire concept might have to be revised.

19

Equipment and Care

Handy Items to Keep in Your Car for Press Photography

Ladder

If you can do so without inconvenience, stow in your car's trunk a three- or four-foot ladder, preferably of light material such as aluminum. You might find it to be highly useful on occasion.

Besides giving you height at a fence or in a crowd, a ladder will allow you to obtain unusual angles that can surprise and delight the newspaper reader. The mind is often caught off guard when the eye sees a view from a position that is not easily attainable. For example, suppose you are photographing a bazaar outside a church where there is a long table and people examining objects on it. If you place your ladder at one end of the table and shoot downward with a wide-angle lens, you can get a sweeping view that takes in the length of the table, an interesting angle of the people from above, and the church in the background. This type of angle can also make a classroom scene interesting by showing individual

A small, light ladder is a good item to keep in your car for obtaining unusual angles.

students more fully than they would appear if they blocked each other while you were taking a picture at their level.

Taking pictures from above of people featured in the foreground against backgrounds such as houses and stores often produces a more dynamic picture than from straight ahead. In addition, they can be looking directly in front of them and not be staring directly into the camera, but under it. (Pictures taken from below also have this advantage, with the subject looking over the lens.)

Floodlights and Spotlights

If you have occasional calls for head shots, being able to set up studio lighting quickly with two or three floods and a spot can give you results of high quality rather than functional photos with flat outdoor or flash lighting.

If color is sometimes called for, you can use blue floods instead of regular photofloods. Blue bulbs can also be used for black-and-white. Otherwise, conversion filters for daylight-tungsten can be kept in your camera bag. Blue light for daylight film with the use of a white bulb in the background can, for effect, add reddish tone to your photo, as a blue bulb can add a bluish tinge to tungsten lighting and film.

Maps

If you cover a large area comprised of many townships, boroughs, or counties, you should have street maps of each section so that you can quickly pinpoint and find a specific place, either for spot news on spec or for feature or other assignments.

Camera Bags

Camera bags are available in a variety of types and sizes. They come with over-the-shoulder straps and/or handles, in canvas, leather, plastic, and cloth, and most are compartmentalized. There are also suitcase-type hand-carrying bags. Some have foam rubber pads with cutout sections for specific equipment.

The most popular means of transporting equipment seems to be the shoulder bag. My preference, though, is a carrying bag with a handle. I find that it provides the additional room I need for my camera bodies, lenses, film, spare batteries, plunger, filters, and other odds and ends. I use a bag with a shoulder strap for my flash equipment. With this combination arrangement I am able to locate easily and quickly the accessories I need, and I can leave my flash equipment in my car if it is not required.

But, like most other aspects of press photography, you will

have to find out for yourself what is the best way for you to transport your own equipment.

Caring for Your Equipment/Repair

The most important maintenance task is to check the batteries of your camera, flash, motor drive, or whatever other equipment is battery-operated. Also, always keep spare batteries on hand.

Lenses should be cleaned regularly with proper tissues and fluids, following the manufacturers' instructions carefully.

Constantly check to make sure your equipment is operating properly. If it isn't, camera store personnel, by checking it out and examining the quality of negatives you are getting, can usually help solve mechanical problems that may occur. They can also ship your equipment back to the manufacturer or tell you the best way to handle this yourself.

In some large cities there are shops that deal specifically with camera repair. These can be located easily through camera dealers.

Toting Camera Equipment

A light hand truck or luggage carrier can come in handy for assignments or spec situations that require covering a large area during which much picture taking must be done and more than a minimal amount of equipment must be carted.

Insurance

Your homeowner's policy should cover your camera equipment. However, it is best to check with your insurance company or agent about what constitutes comprehensive coverage of photographic apparatus. It is usually best that the company have a list containing the name of each item, any serial numbers, and the cost of replacement.

A luggage hand truck can relieve you of the chore of lugging heavy or excessive equipment.

Certain companies specialize in insuring photographic equipment, and a few inquiring phone calls to representatives in the field should put you in touch with the proper contact in your area.

20

Spin-off Sales

Beyond Newspaper Markets

Amassing a growing collection of pictures of great variety can pay off in future sales. Any number of publications may be interested in buying some of these pictures from you.

Local and regional magazines, your chamber of commerce, Sunday newspaper magazines, trade magazines, and, if the subject is strong enough, popular magazines and even news magazines are sales possibilities.

Market lists for purchasers of photographs are available in the monthly photographers' and writers' trade magazines that appear on the newsstands, in supermarkets, and in bookstores. These can be obtained by subscription or seen in libraries.

Annual books specializing in photography markets are also available for purchase and can also be found on some library shelves, as can books written specifically about this subject. The market listings provided by these publications supply editors' names, addresses, and such facts as the needs of their particular markets and what they pay for pictures.

Trade magazines and house organs, which purchase pictures from professionals, semiprofessionals, and amateurs, cover a wide range of subject matter.

On occasion, after publication of an auto accident picture, an attorney or insurance company will contact a photographer to buy copies for legal use. In fact, the photographer might wish to take the initiative by contacting the persons involved. However, you should investigate the possibility of being required to appear as a witness in court, depending on the law regarding this in your area or state. It might be a wise move, before releasing such pictures for sale, to obtain in writing from the purchaser an agreement that you will appear, if necessary—but only on terms that you deem reasonable at that time, involving financial compensation for your time and expenses.

Stock photo companies are another market. These services file away millions of photographs in various categories—in black-and-white and color—submitted by photographers, many of whom are not full-time, from across the country and around the world. Sales are made to a wide range of markets, such as magazine and book publishers and advertising agencies. Standard payment is about 50 percent of each sale. Information on stock companies can be found in most of the books just noted.

There are innumerable other markets, such as calendar companies, greeting card publishers, public relations firms, and record companies.

Tear Sheets

In order to promote yourself with your work, you should keep samples of all published pictures. I keep copies of my work, as a record, by cutting out the photos and their captions, as well as the accompanying articles. I mount these on sheets of 8½- x 11-inch bond paper by their corners with two-sided sticky tape.

Sometimes the photo or layout is larger than 8½ x 11 inches. In such cases I cut out the portion—or the entire page—I wish to save, fasten down one part of it, and fold the rest so that its compact dimensions are under 8½ x 11 inches. I then keep these in piles in chronological order, divided by year.

In this form, they may be duplicated easily by a photo copier when you wish to send them out as samples of your work. If the size you wish to copy is larger than 8½ x 11 inches, each folded section can be copied separately, then taped together, and the total copy itself folded for submission.

Of course, it's a good idea to get as many extra clippings as you can for future use to save photocopying expense. Newspapers temporarily retain a good number of extra past issues to be used by reporters and photographers for filing, review, and other purposes. You should obtain what you need from them as soon as possible—before they are discarded.

Portfolio

Once your work begins to see print, whether in your high school newspaper or in a local tabloid—or even before—it is a good idea to put together a neat, compact collection of samples to show to newspaper editors.

You may, in fact, have in your location other potential markets for your skills. These could be advertising agencies, stores, real estate brokers—any number of businesses that, although they do not use press photography–style photographs, can still make use of your abilities.

To display your work effectively and impressively, you might buy an artist's portfolio—a briefcase zippered on three sides, with handles, that opens like a book and contains glassine pages. These pages range from 8 x 11 inches to several times that size.

In this portfolio, you should display photographs that you feel show your talent. If it contains published pictures, show your original prints alongside those newspaper clippings.

Showcase Packages

Should you wish to submit work to a magazine or other market—either as a finished product, or simply as a proposal—it is a good idea to include a package of photocopies of samples of your work that represent your talent well, in addition to published pictures that are in the same tenor as those used by the editor to whom you are proposing your idea.

Always be certain to enclose a SASE (self-addressed stamped envelope) for the return of your clippings. This serves two purposes. It, of course, ensures the return of your material, which is difficult or perhaps expensive to replace. But it also makes it convenient for a busy editor to respond to you quickly by tossing a note in with your material. And, since you made the response easy, the note might just show an inclination to be receptive.

Résumés

Put together a list of your accomplishments in photography, noting everything you have done—from contributing to your high school newspaper to local library photo exhibits or other accomplishments. As your credits increase, add to this list. A copy of your résumé can be left following an interview, and it can be included in your showcase package mailings.

Business Cards

It is always worthwhile to have business cards printed and to carry them with you. When you are covering a spot-news event or you are on assignment and people see a professional photographer at work, they sometimes decide to ask to use your services on the spot.

Occasionally, someone will ask about getting copies of the pictures you are taking. If you are on assignment, the negatives, of course, do not belong to you; however, you can suggest that those interested contact the newspaper. But if you are working on spec, an opportunity like this can provide extra income.

You will usually be rushed at a news event, and being able to whip out a business card will allow you to provide instant identification for someone who wants to get in touch with you later. It also shows professionalism.

21

Organizations, Awards, and Grants

Organizations for Press Photographers

The most important professional group for photojournalists is the National Press Photographers Association (NPPA), founded more than thirty-five years ago. This organization—whose membership includes, besides newspaper photographers, camera people from television journalism—is subdivided into regions that have their own directors, as well as into state chapters.

NPPA is a highly respected and influential association whose activities include monthly and annual news photo clipping and audiovisual tape contests for its membership, a regular magazine and other publications, workshops, seminars, and national committees that deal in such areas as freedom of information, education, joint media, police-press relations, portfolio critique, television, and scholarships. There is an annual business and education seminar. Student memberships are available, as well as information regarding photographic internships. Additional membership benefits include a press card, a general identification card that can be used in a car, and other items and services.

The American Society of Magazine Photographers— formerly The Society of Photographers in Communications— or ASMP, extends beyond journalism into the fields of advertising, book publishing, industrial photography, TV, and other areas of commercial visual communication. One of its primary purposes is to protect the economic well-being of its members by setting rates. ASMP also deals with ethics and legal matters.

The current mailing addresses and names of officers to whom you can write for information regarding these and other photography organizations can be obtained from the latest annual editions of the previously mentioned publications dealing with such listings.

Photojournalism Awards

Many awards are given annually to press photographers. These range from the Pulitzer Prize to gifts of recognition from various fields, such as medicine and sports, and from companies, associations, and other dedicated groups.

Information about these competitions and how to enter your work is available through newspapers, photography organizations, colleges, and other sources. Application forms and related information can usually be obtained by writing to the appropriate award committees. If you are unable to get mailing addresses, your local librarian should be of help.

Foundation Grants in Photography

Photojournalism has become more and more recognized as an art form. Photography exhibits and even art galleries are devoting more space than ever before to this genre of photography.

Photography resulting from grant monies is increasingly reflecting a visual journalistic viewpoint on people and human drama.

The National Endowment for the Arts offers aspiring photographers an opportunity to obtain grants for support of their talents and ambitions. Other organizations, such as the John Simon Guggenheim Memorial Foundation, may also be applied to for funds. In addition, there are local and state foundations that provide financial support for photographers.

Information regarding grants from these and other organizations can be obtained from books and other literature at most libraries, through photography magazines, and at colleges and universities.

22

Press Photography as a Full-time Job

Although the purpose of this guide is to provide information regarding freelance press photography, some readers might eventually wish to consider employment as newspaper photographers.

There are many advantages, of course, to being on a payroll as a newspaper photographer, the primary one being a steady paycheck plus free hospital and life insurance, pension, and other standard company benefits. These are received whether or not your pictures are always used. But there are also other benefits accruing to a staff photographer.

A full-time press photographer is supplied with free film and has use of the newspaper's darkroom and its equipment, chemicals, paper, and other supplies.

Some newspapers provide the photographer with a car and also pay for its insurance, service, repairs, and gas. Others pay their employed photographers on a per-mile basis for mileage driven in their personal cars on assignments.

209

There are newspapers whose policy is not only to cover the cost of insurance and repair of their photographers' camera equipment, but to pay each photographer, in addition to salary, a monthly amount based on use of that equipment. This may be done, for example, in thirty-six monthly payments over a three-year period, based on the total value of the photographer's apparatus. Still other newspapers provide their own camera equipment for the photographer's use.

In addition, newspapers of substantial circulation often have technical people on staff to do the photofinishing.

Scanners are also provided by some newspapers—and, in some cases, editors keep in touch with their photographers by CB radio.

Additional income may, in certain instances, be forthcoming to the employed photographer whose photographs are sent out over the wire to other newspapers.

Newspapers are, for the most part, obligated to defend their employees in legal matters regarding freedom of the press should a problem arise; for example, over whether it was proper for a photographer to take certain pictures. In order to maintain journalistic integrity, a newspaper publisher must sometimes even fight for an employee. A freelance photographer, often acting on his or her own, however, may not necessarily be a liability to a sometime employer.

Besides offering security, a newspaper job as a staff photographer provides an almost daily opportunity to deal with new and challenging situations, constant occasions to meet interesting people, and the stimulation of working regularly with many talented associates. And, most importantly, the staff photographer's steadily appearing work is a constant reminder of accomplishment.

23

Becoming Established as a Freelance Photojournalist

Of all photographic fields, press photography, or photojournalism, is probably one of the most challenging and demanding. Other kinds, such as studio portrait, wedding, and model, require development of a certain basic routine regarding subject, film, lighting, and processing that, once established, is used constantly.

The press photographer, on the other hand, rushes to a news or feature event never knowing fully what light conditions to expect, what the people to be photographed will be like, and sometimes even how many will be there and who they are. Neither has the press photographer any idea of whether the people with whom he will be dealing will be cooperative or resistant. Any obstacles—physical, legal, or other—are usually discovered on arrival, at the same time the job must be done.

Immediately after reaching a scene and assessing it, the press photographer not only must decide what should be photographed to capture the essence of that news story, but

211

also must consider all the technical aspects of putting it on film. This requires that you pay attention to details ranging from lighting and angle to the finished prints. Is the existing light satisfactory? Will it have to be supplemented? If so, with floods, flash, both, other? What film should be used? Should it be push-processed? Which lens or lenses should be used? Which subject or subjects should be photographed? From what viewpoint? What, if anything, should be in the background? Should the background be in or out of focus?

Sometimes there are other problems with which the photographer must deal: how to get permission to take pictures on a scene; how to convince a person to pose; how to manage to get people to allow more time to take pictures; or, conversely, how to speed up the picture-taking session to make a deadline.

How does an aspiring freelance photojournalist break into the field? And, once started, how does the press photographer advance? First of all, in order to deal with the myriad aspects of photojournalism, the photographer must possess the requisite knowledge, skill, and experience. All of this is attainable if, along with talent, you have a willingness to work hard and a constant desire for improvement.

As in any other field, it is usually necessary to prove yourself through a step-by-step process. Naturally, as in any other field, you can take shortcuts in press photography. And luck, as with many occupations, also figures into the photojournalist's destiny.

Sometimes, covering events regularly in your area, on your own, can get you almost instant recognition as a good news photographer and help you bypass a more conventional gradual climb upward. But the most logical and practical means of advance in press photography is to begin with your local tabloids. These publications pay little or nothing, but they give you the opportunity to get your work into print. They are usually single-person operations, always on a tight budget. But, to your advantage, it is not often that a photographer who can turn out good work approaches these editors.

Local publications have many area advertisers whom the editors want to photograph in their new or ongoing establishments; however, photographers are not always available to take these mundane pictures. There are business association meetings, groundbreakings, local news feature events, school happenings, and many other activities that are waiting to be photographed.

Once you can get a selection of pictures published in these newspapers, you can use them for a portfolio for eventual submission to a larger-area newspaper. Then you can build your portfolio further and try to get a hearing at a nearby metropolitan newspaper. You may be fortunate by having in your area a number of competing newspapers.

Most importantly, the sooner you become knowledgeable about the basics of photography and can turn out adequate— and better than adequate—photographs, the greater the possibility that you will be trusted by editors, especially for assignments.

How do you learn the basics—and the more complicated aspects—of photography? There are a number of ways: through practical picture-taking experience obtained by trial and error; by reading photography books and magazines; by taking courses in the subject; and by any combination of the above.

Many courses in photography should be available to you locally. You can find them at schools offering adult education and at community colleges. Some camera stores can advise you on classes given near your home, and some even offer courses of their own. Complete curricula, along with course credit, are available at some institutions that focus specifically on photography. And colleges and universities, recognizing the growing need for teaching photography, are now filling that need and even offering degrees in photography. In addition, mail order courses are available.

Once you are into freelancing, it is most important that you keep up with the latest technical developments in photography regarding techniques, equipment, chemicals, paper, and as many other aspects of the field as can help you in this line of endeavor. Books and magazines heralding these advancements constantly flood the marketplace and show up in libraries.

Why do newspapers use freelancers? Although many newspapers maintain a staff of photographers, they depend on freelancers to bring in the pictures they cannot get because of the impossibility of covering a large area. Besides spot news, this includes assignments that their own photographers are too busy to schedule. There is usually a budget allowance to cover this expense.

The newspaper benefits in a number of ways by buying from freelancers. When purchasing freelance spot news photos submitted on spec, the newspaper usually purchases only those pictures used and/or invited to the newsroom—or possibly pays a minimal amount for those not published. On both spot news and assignments, the newspaper also has use of the freelancer's private automobile on a per-mile basis, when otherwise it might have to pay for a car and expenses for a staffer, cab fares, or rental fee for an automobile for a full day no matter how long it is used.

Additional benefits of using freelance pictures are that important spot news at various locations in the newspaper's circulation area is covered, and the readers at those points are pleased with having on-the-spot shots taken where they live. As a result, they become interested in purchasing the newspaper regularly from a newsstand or in having it delivered. This, in turn, results in increased circulation—followed often by an increase in advertising.

Therefore, full photographic coverage is advantageous to photographer and publisher.

In general, then, freelancing benefits both the employer and the photographer. While the newspaper need not maintain the photographer on an expensive full-time basis, and need only pay for the time that the freelancer is actively working on a photographic project, the freelancer is free between assignment times to pursue work with other newspapers and in other areas of photography—in a convenient, self-planned schedule.

Most large newspapers operate basically on a seven-day-per-week basis. Because of this, especially if you are in an area with a number of competing newspapers, there is a continuous opportunity for sales, as well as the choice of taking time off at your own convenience.

A freelance photojournalist should be constantly reachable. A good way to be on call, if someone cannot always be by your telephone to take sudden assignments, is to use an answering service or machine. A most useful machine is the remote type that you can "beep" from a phone anywhere in order to obtain your messages. If you carry your camera equipment with you in your car, you can, if necessary, go immediately to the scene of a news event.

The competition in freelance newspaper photography is keen. Editors look for creative pictures that are "different." You must set high standards for yourself—and stick to them.

I have heard comments about commonplace pictures—taken of such subjects as awards, groundbreakings, and even less formal situations—that referred to "grip-and-grin" or "line-up-and-shoot" photographs taken by "shuttersnappers," as well as other disparaging comments.

To rise above the majority of your competitors you must be a thinking photographer, avoiding the usual commonly taken, trite poses and scenes. Constantly look for new angles and fresh visual expression—as a writer looks to find a "voice." Try to develop your own individual style, with a personal—and honest—interpretation of today's world of growing complexity.

Each photographer has a unique outlook on life and either consciously or unconsciously allows only that viewpoint through the camera lens. Study the classic photos of "name" photojournalists. Carefully analyze newspaper photographs that carry credit lines. You will note an individuality in the work of most photographers, no matter how wide-ranging the subjects photographed.

Whenever possible, avoid sameness. Avoid copying what has already been done. Always look for the new, the unusual. Once you learn the ground rules of picture composition, make every possible effort to be original. Give the editors reason to buy your freelance work—every time you shoot a roll of film.

Index